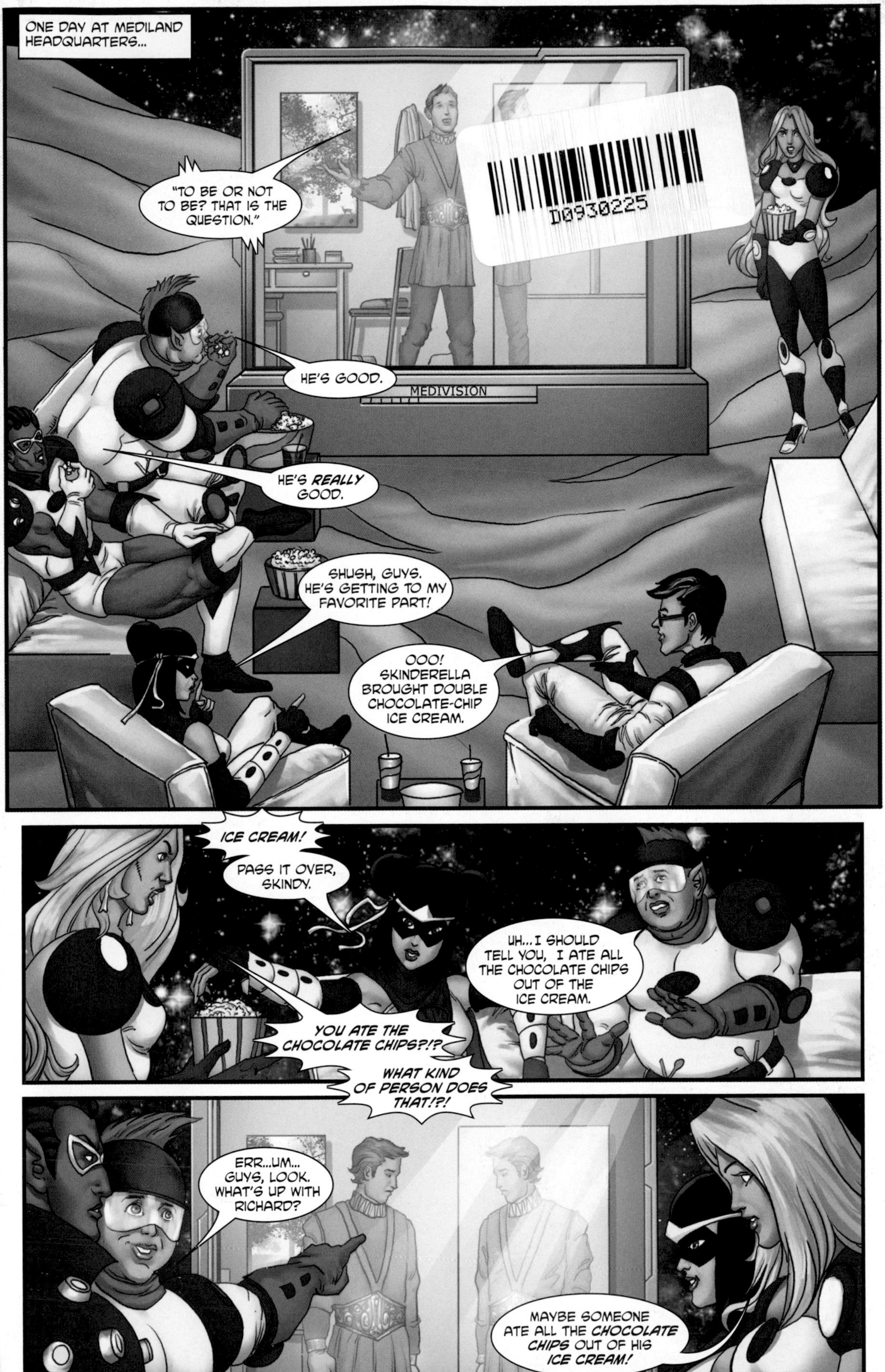

ONE DAY AT MEDILAND HEADQUARTERS...
"TO BE OR NOT TO BE? THAT IS THE QUESTION."
HE'S GOOD.
MEDIVISION
HE'S *REALLY* GOOD.
SHUSH, GUYS. HE'S GETTING TO MY FAVORITE PART!
OOO! SKINDERELLA BROUGHT DOUBLE CHOCOLATE-CHIP ICE CREAM.
ICE CREAM!
PASS IT OVER, SKINDY.
UH... I SHOULD TELL YOU, I ATE ALL THE CHOCOLATE CHIPS OUT OF THE ICE CREAM.
YOU ATE THE CHOCOLATE CHIPS?!?
WHAT KIND OF PERSON DOES THAT!?!
ERR...UM... GUYS, LOOK. WHAT'S UP WITH RICHARD?
MAYBE SOMEONE ATE ALL THE *CHOCOLATE CHIPS* OUT OF HIS *ICE CREAM!*

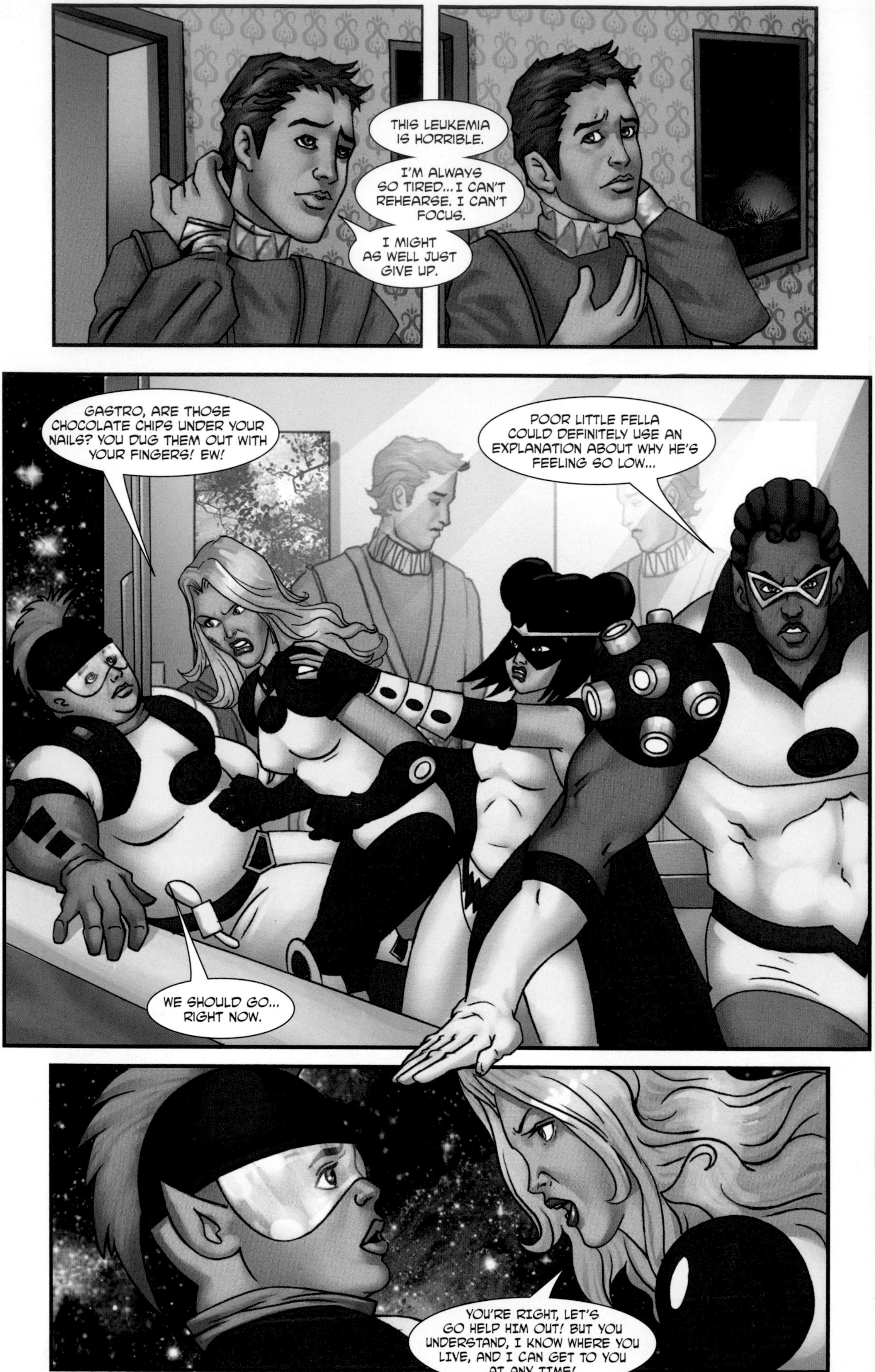
THIS LEUKEMIA IS HORRIBLE.
I'M ALWAYS SO TIRED... I CAN'T REHEARSE. I CAN'T FOCUS.
I MIGHT AS WELL JUST GIVE UP.
GASTRO, ARE THOSE CHOCOLATE CHIPS UNDER YOUR NAILS? YOU DUG THEM OUT WITH YOUR FINGERS! EW!
POOR LITTLE FELLA COULD DEFINITELY USE AN EXPLANATION ABOUT WHY HE'S FEELING SO LOW...
WE SHOULD GO... RIGHT NOW.
YOU'RE RIGHT, LET'S GO HELP HIM OUT! BUT YOU UNDERSTAND, I KNOW WHERE YOU LIVE, AND I CAN GET TO YOU AT ANY TIME!

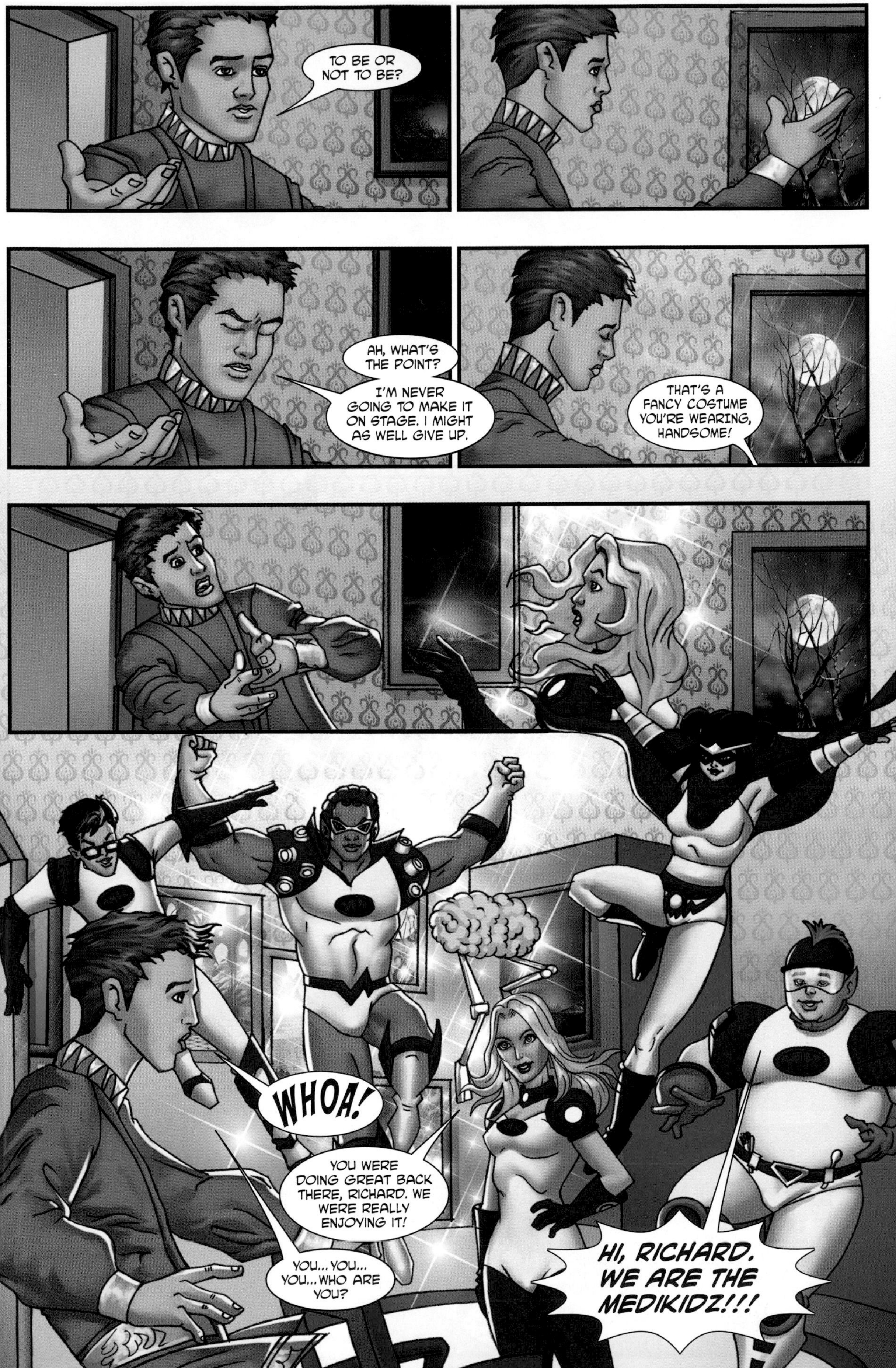
TO BE OR NOT TO BE?
AH, WHAT'S THE POINT?
I'M NEVER GOING TO MAKE IT ON STAGE. I MIGHT AS WELL GIVE UP.
THAT'S A FANCY COSTUME YOU'RE WEARING, HANDSOME!
WHOA!
YOU WERE DOING GREAT BACK THERE, RICHARD. WE WERE REALLY ENJOYING IT!
YOU... YOU... YOU... WHO ARE YOU?
HI, RICHARD. WE ARE THE MEDIKIDZ!!!

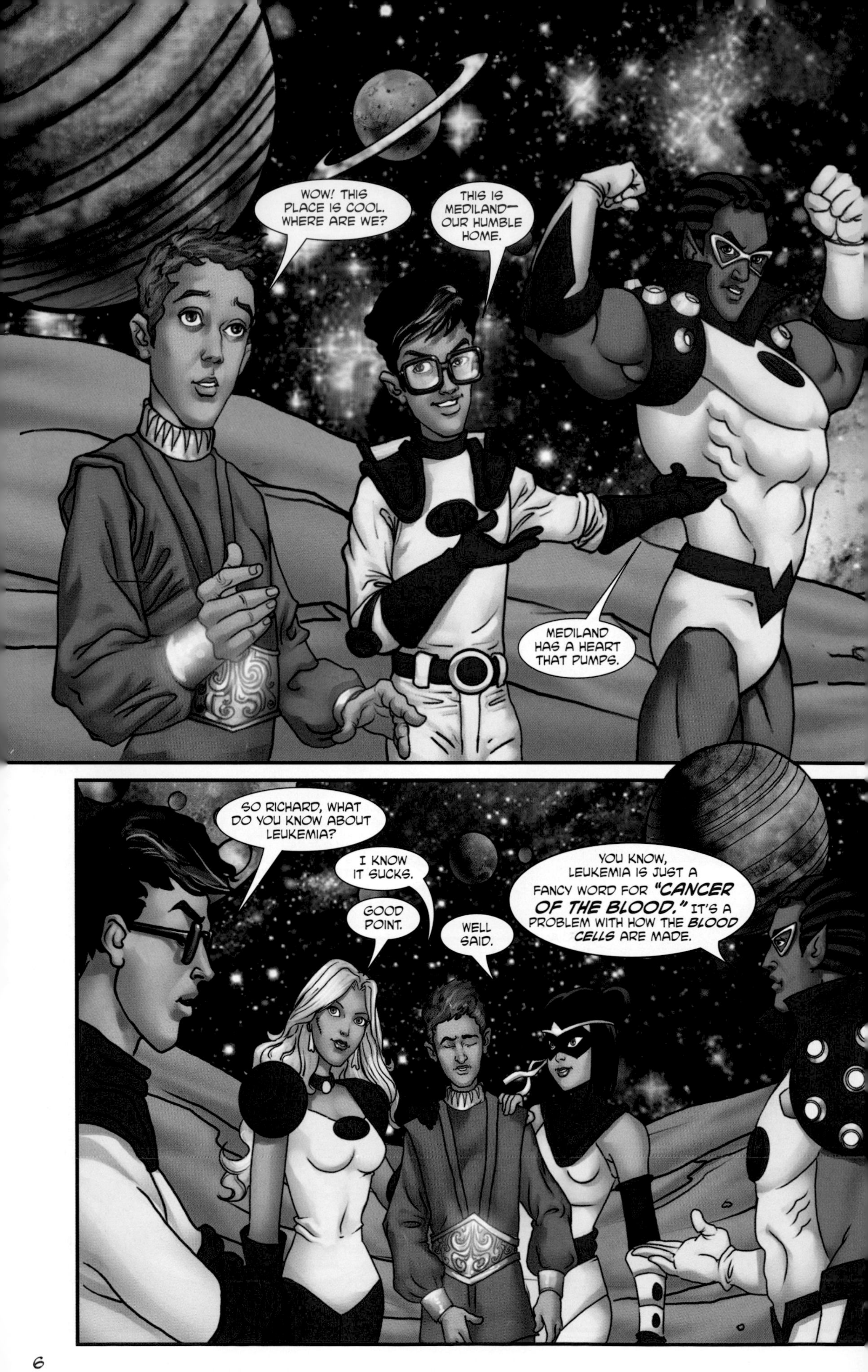
WOW! THIS PLACE IS COOL. WHERE ARE WE?
THIS IS MEDILAND— OUR HUMBLE HOME.
MEDILAND HAS A HEART THAT PUMPS.
SO RICHARD, WHAT DO YOU KNOW ABOUT LEUKEMIA?
I KNOW IT SUCKS.
GOOD POINT.
WELL SAID.
YOU KNOW, LEUKEMIA IS JUST A FANCY WORD FOR ***"CANCER OF THE BLOOD."*** IT'S A PROBLEM WITH HOW THE *BLOOD CELLS* ARE MADE.

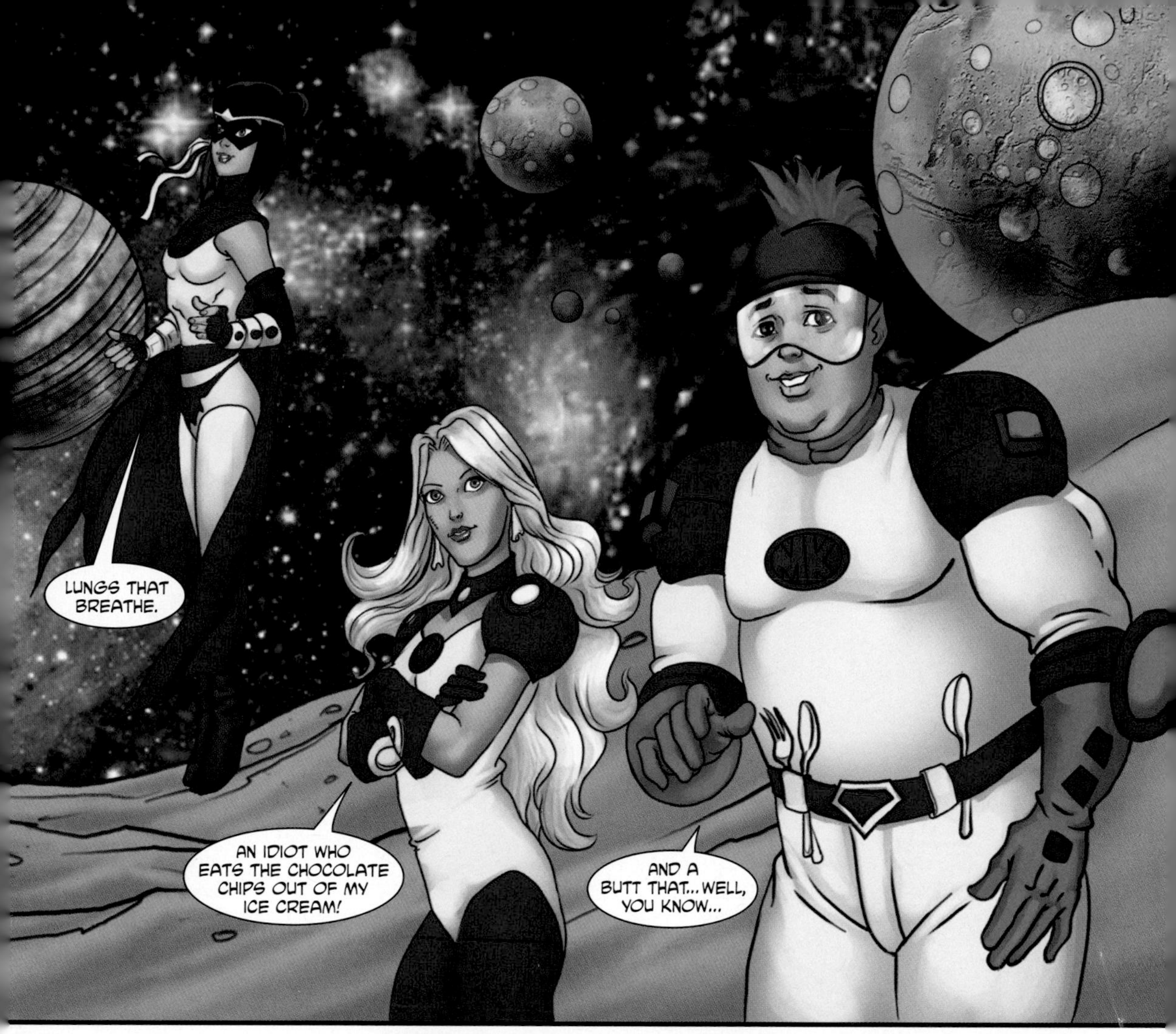
LUNGS THAT BREATHE.
AN IDIOT WHO EATS THE CHOCOLATE CHIPS OUT OF MY ICE CREAM!
AND A BUTT THAT... WELL, YOU KNOW...

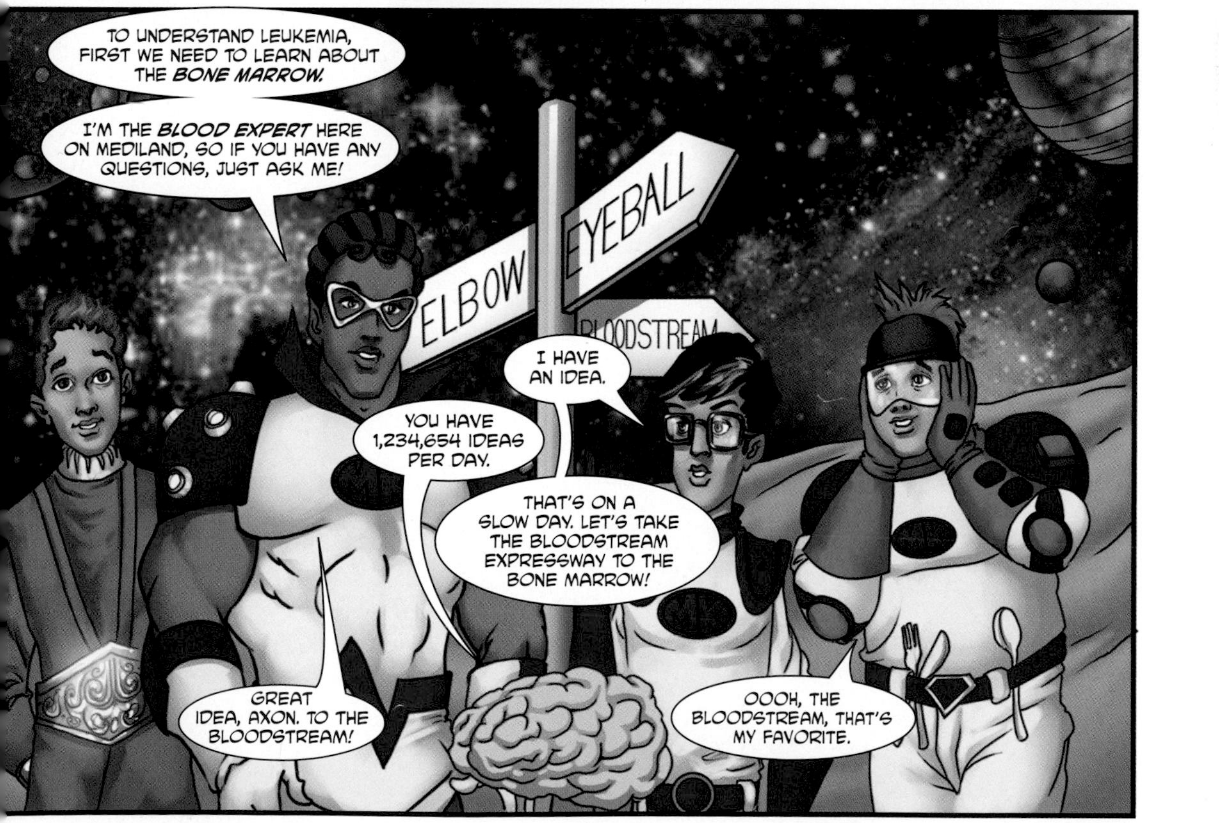
TO UNDERSTAND LEUKEMIA, FIRST WE NEED TO LEARN ABOUT THE *BONE MARROW.*
I'M THE *BLOOD EXPERT* HERE ON MEDILAND, SO IF YOU HAVE ANY QUESTIONS, JUST ASK ME!
ELBOW
EYEBALL
BLOODSTREAM
I HAVE AN IDEA.
YOU HAVE 1,234,654 IDEAS PER DAY.
THAT'S ON A SLOW DAY. LET'S TAKE THE BLOODSTREAM EXPRESSWAY TO THE BONE MARROW!
GREAT IDEA, AXON. TO THE BLOODSTREAM!
OOOH, THE BLOODSTREAM, THAT'S MY FAVORITE.

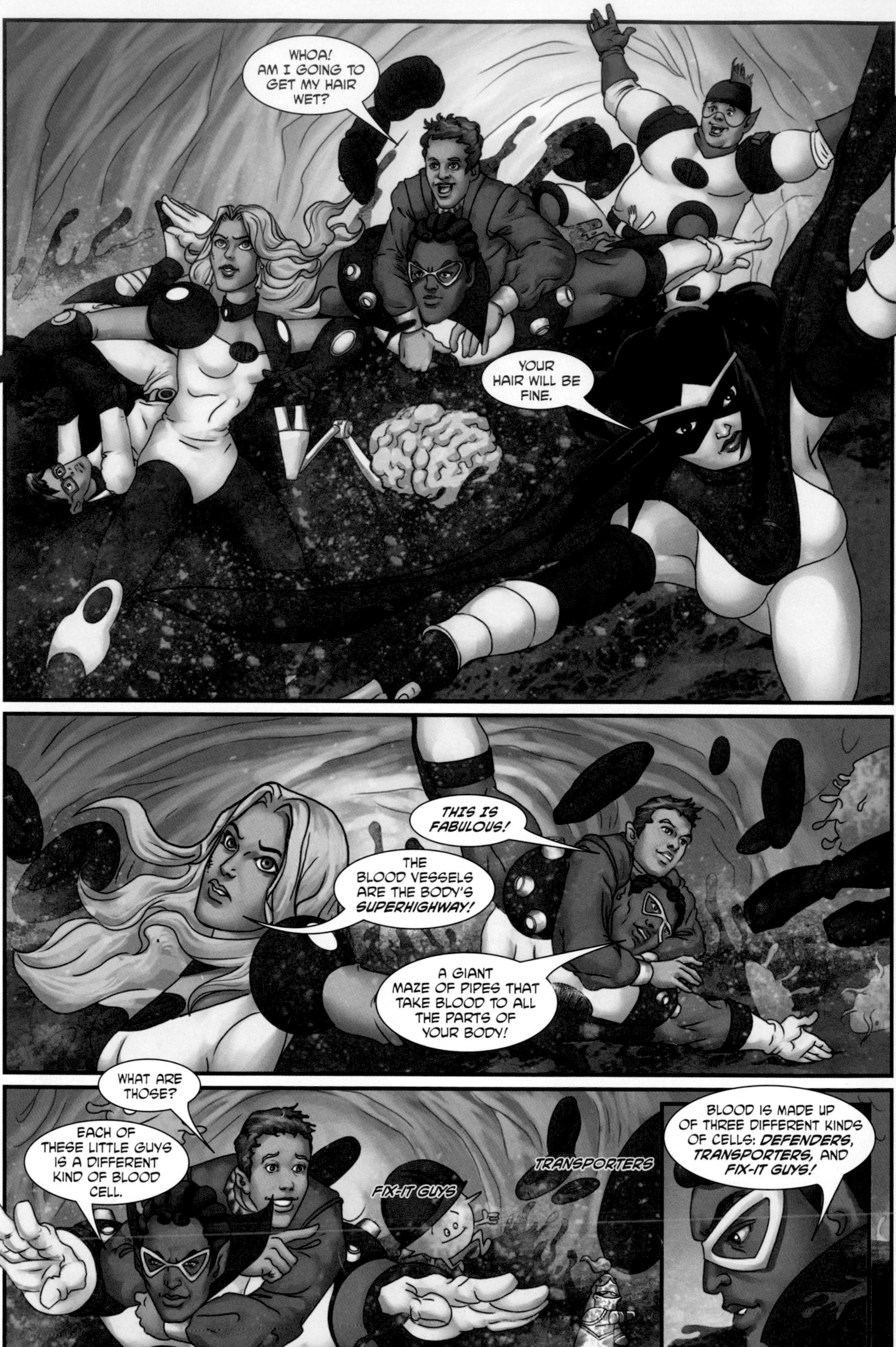

WHOA! AM I GOING TO GET MY HAIR WET?
YOUR HAIR WILL BE FINE.
THIS IS FABULOUS!
THE BLOOD VESSELS ARE THE BODY'S SUPERHIGHWAY!
A GIANT MAZE OF PIPES THAT TAKE BLOOD TO ALL THE PARTS OF YOUR BODY!
WHAT ARE THOSE?
EACH OF THESE LITTLE GUYS IS A DIFFERENT KIND OF BLOOD CELL.
FIX-IT GUYS
TRANSPORTERS
DEFENDERS
BLOOD IS MADE UP OF THREE DIFFERENT KINDS OF CELLS: DEFENDERS, TRANSPORTERS, AND FIX-IT GUYS!

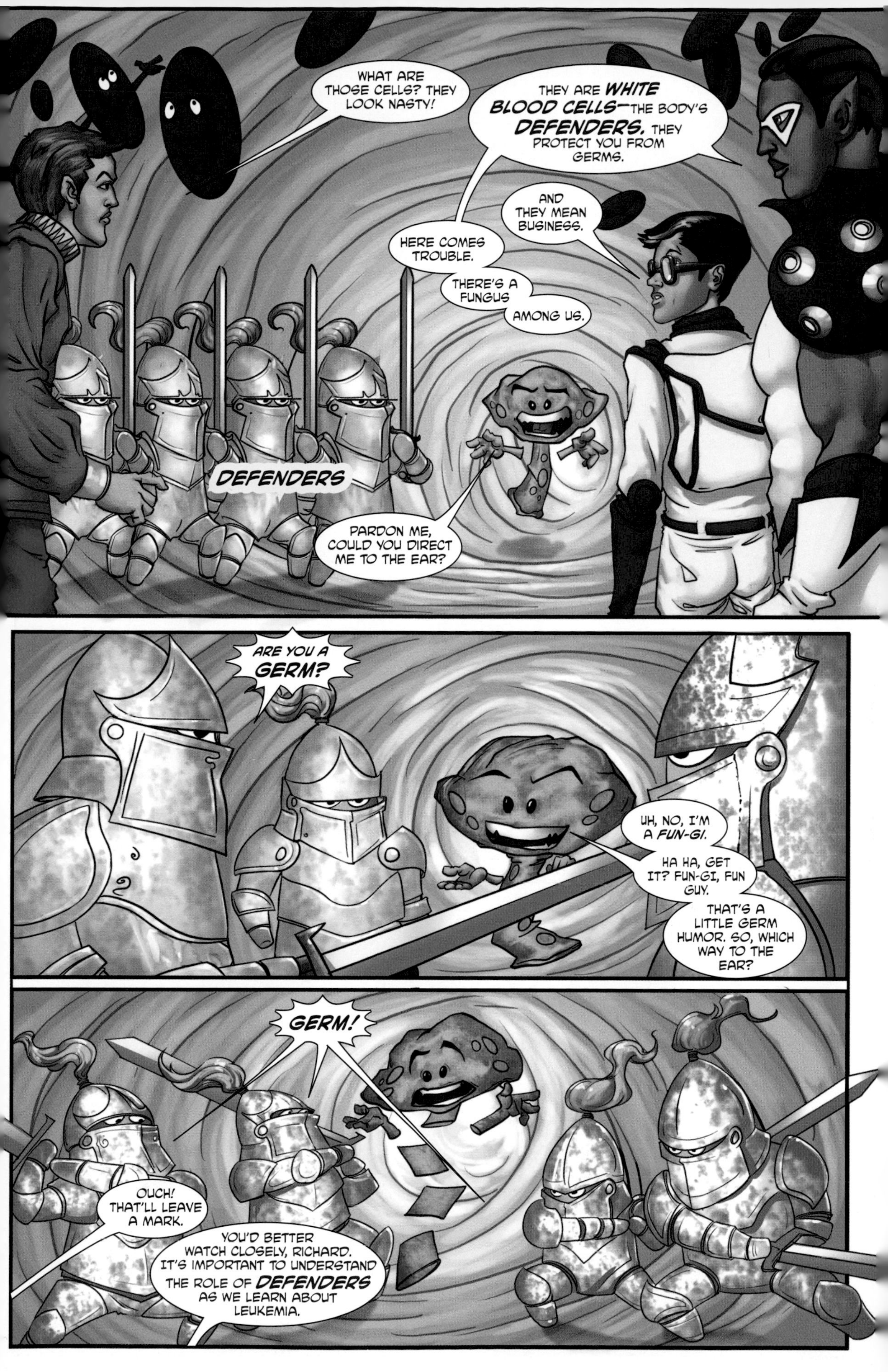
WHAT ARE THOSE CELLS? THEY LOOK NASTY!
THEY ARE WHITE BLOOD CELLS—THE BODY'S DEFENDERS. THEY PROTECT YOU FROM GERMS.
AND THEY MEAN BUSINESS.
HERE COMES TROUBLE.
THERE'S A FUNGUS
AMONG US.
DEFENDERS
PARDON ME, COULD YOU DIRECT ME TO THE EAR?
ARE YOU A GERM?
UH, NO, I'M A FUN-GI.
HA HA, GET IT? FUN-GI, FUN GUY.
THAT'S A LITTLE GERM HUMOR. SO, WHICH WAY TO THE EAR?
GERM!
OUCH! THAT'LL LEAVE A MARK.
YOU'D BETTER WATCH CLOSELY, RICHARD. IT'S IMPORTANT TO UNDERSTAND THE ROLE OF DEFENDERS AS WE LEARN ABOUT LEUKEMIA.

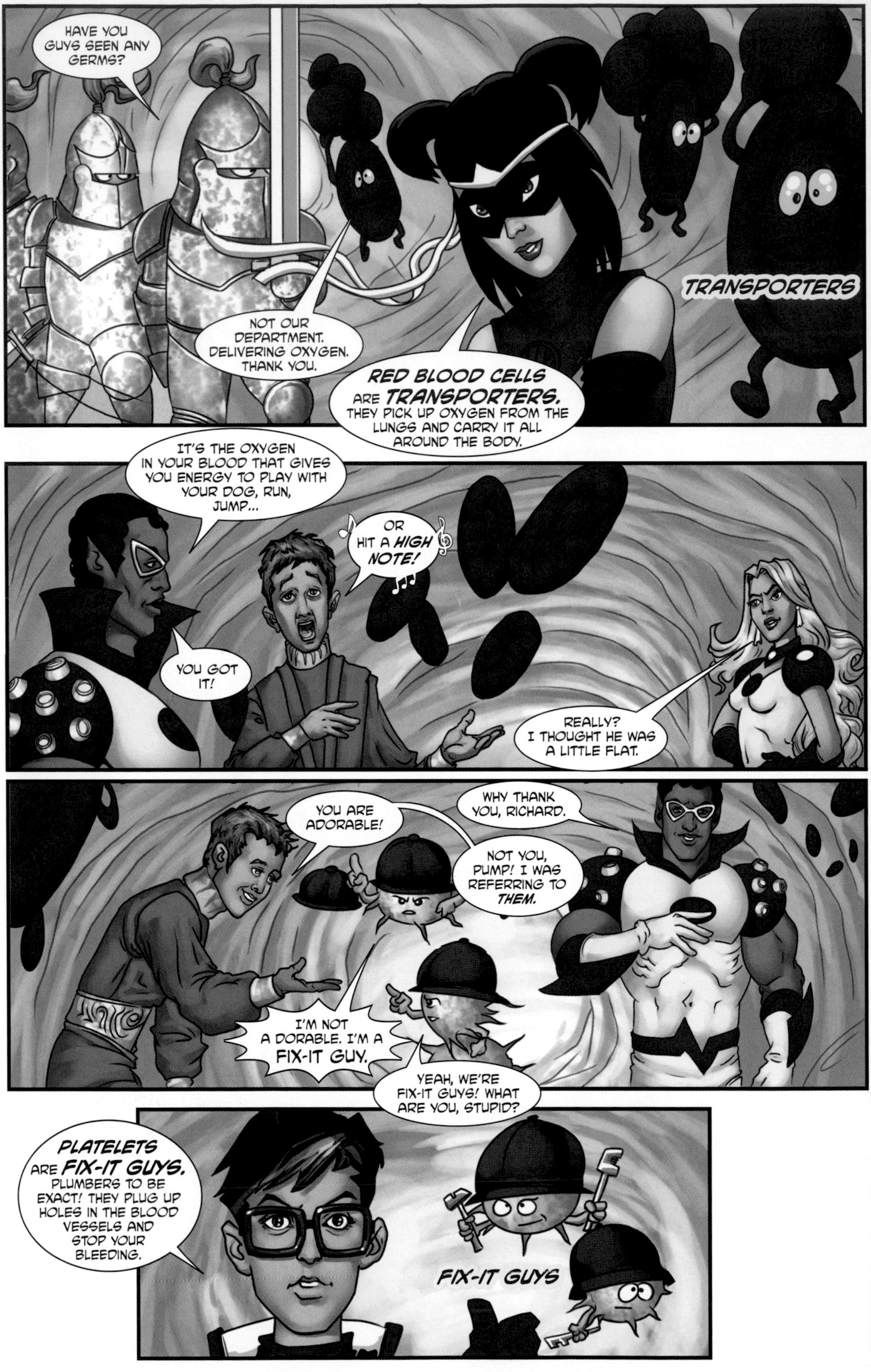

HAVE YOU GUYS SEEN ANY GERMS?
NOT OUR DEPARTMENT. DELIVERING OXYGEN. THANK YOU.
RED BLOOD CELLS ARE TRANSPORTERS. THEY PICK UP OXYGEN FROM THE LUNGS AND CARRY IT ALL AROUND THE BODY.
TRANSPORTERS
IT'S THE OXYGEN IN YOUR BLOOD THAT GIVES YOU ENERGY TO PLAY WITH YOUR DOG, RUN, JUMP...
OR HIT A HIGH NOTE!
YOU GOT IT!
REALLY? I THOUGHT HE WAS A LITTLE FLAT.
YOU ARE ADORABLE!
WHY THANK YOU, RICHARD.
NOT YOU, PUMP! I WAS REFERRING TO THEM.
I'M NOT A DORABLE. I'M A FIX-IT GUY.
YEAH, WE'RE FIX-IT GUYS! WHAT ARE YOU, STUPID?
PLATELETS ARE FIX-IT GUYS. PLUMBERS TO BE EXACT! THEY PLUG UP HOLES IN THE BLOOD VESSELS AND STOP YOUR BLEEDING.
FIX-IT GUYS

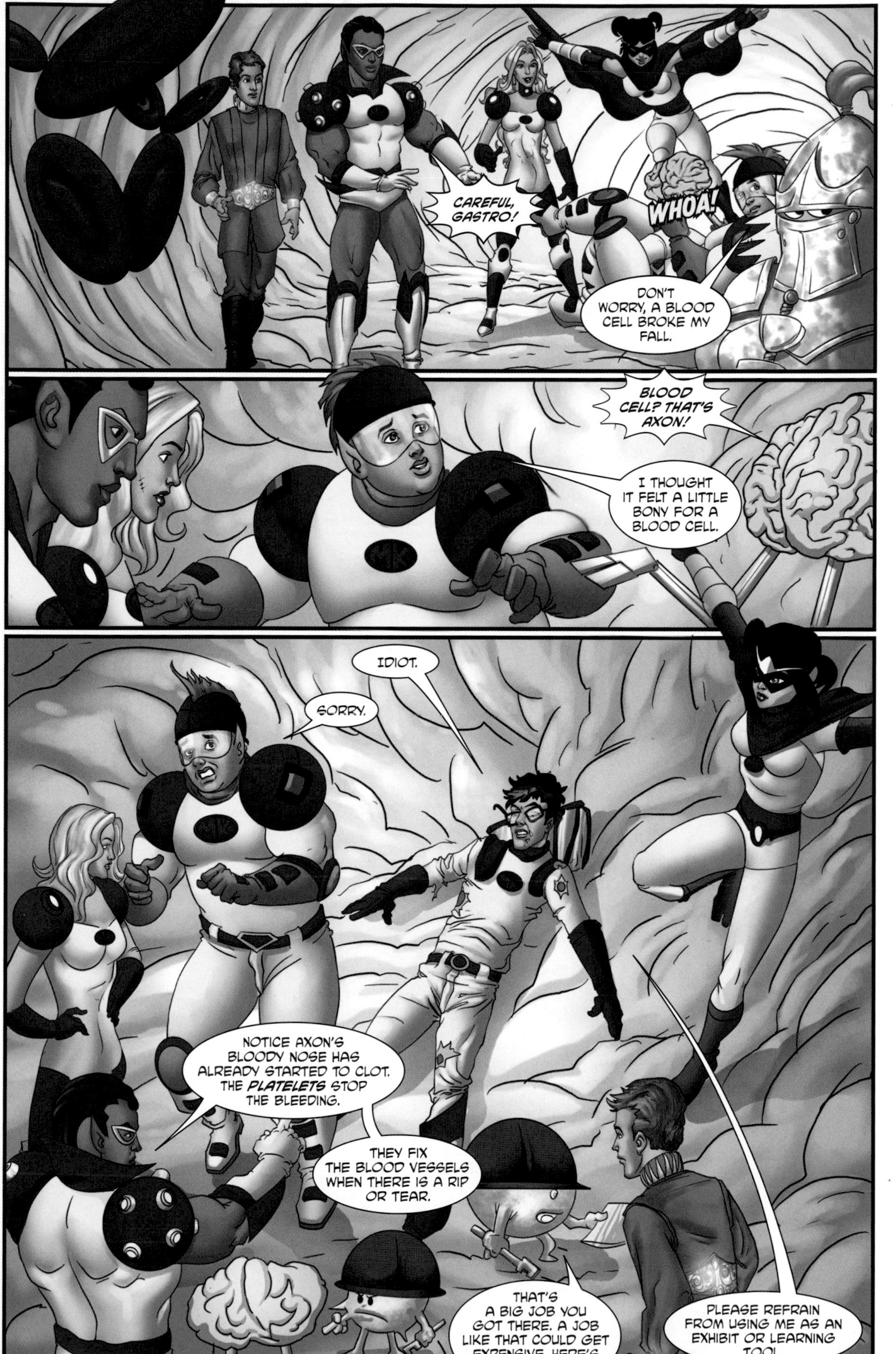
CAREFUL, GASTRO!
WHOA!
DON'T WORRY, A BLOOD CELL BROKE MY FALL.
BLOOD CELL? THAT'S AXON!
I THOUGHT IT FELT A LITTLE BONY FOR A BLOOD CELL.
IDIOT.
SORRY.
NOTICE AXON'S BLOODY NOSE HAS ALREADY STARTED TO CLOT. THE PLATELETS STOP THE BLEEDING.
THEY FIX THE BLOOD VESSELS WHEN THERE IS A RIP OR TEAR.
THAT'S A BIG JOB YOU GOT THERE. A JOB LIKE THAT COULD GET EXPENSIVE. HERE'S OUR ESTIMATE.
PLEASE REFRAIN FROM USING ME AS AN EXHIBIT OR LEARNING TOOL.

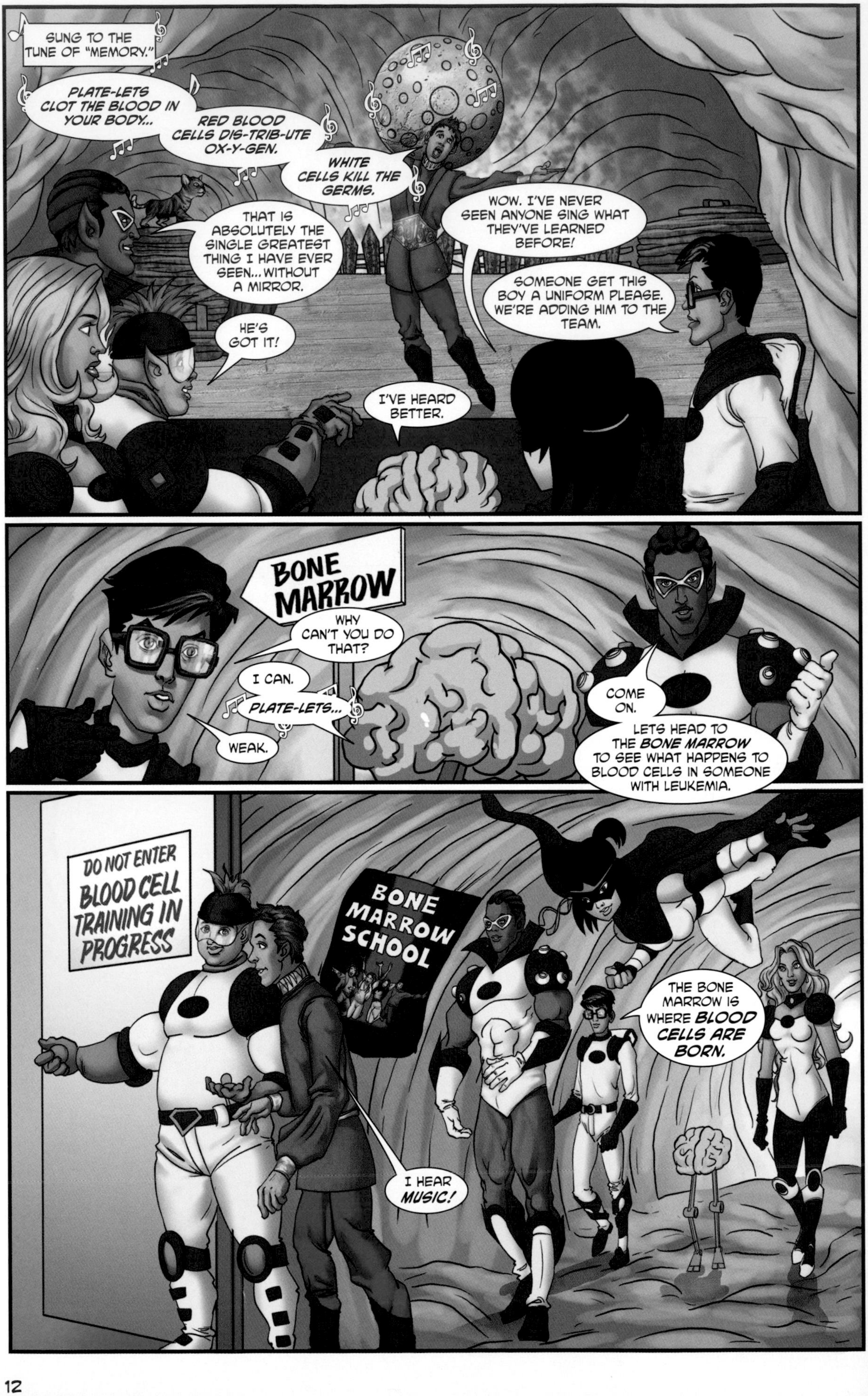
SUNG TO THE TUNE OF "MEMORY."
PLATE-LETS CLOT THE BLOOD IN YOUR BODY...
RED BLOOD CELLS DIS-TRIB-UTE OX-Y-GEN.
WHITE CELLS KILL THE GERMS.
THAT IS ABSOLUTELY THE SINGLE GREATEST THING I HAVE EVER SEEN... WITHOUT A MIRROR.
WOW. I'VE NEVER SEEN ANYONE SING WHAT THEY'VE LEARNED BEFORE!
SOMEONE GET THIS BOY A UNIFORM PLEASE. WE'RE ADDING HIM TO THE TEAM.
HE'S GOT IT!
I'VE HEARD BETTER.
BONE MARROW
WHY CAN'T YOU DO THAT?
I CAN.
PLATE-LETS...
WEAK.
COME ON.
LETS HEAD TO THE BONE MARROW TO SEE WHAT HAPPENS TO BLOOD CELLS IN SOMEONE WITH LEUKEMIA.
DO NOT ENTER BLOOD CELL TRAINING IN PROGRESS
BONE MARROW SCHOOL
THE BONE MARROW IS WHERE BLOOD CELLS ARE BORN.
I HEAR MUSIC!

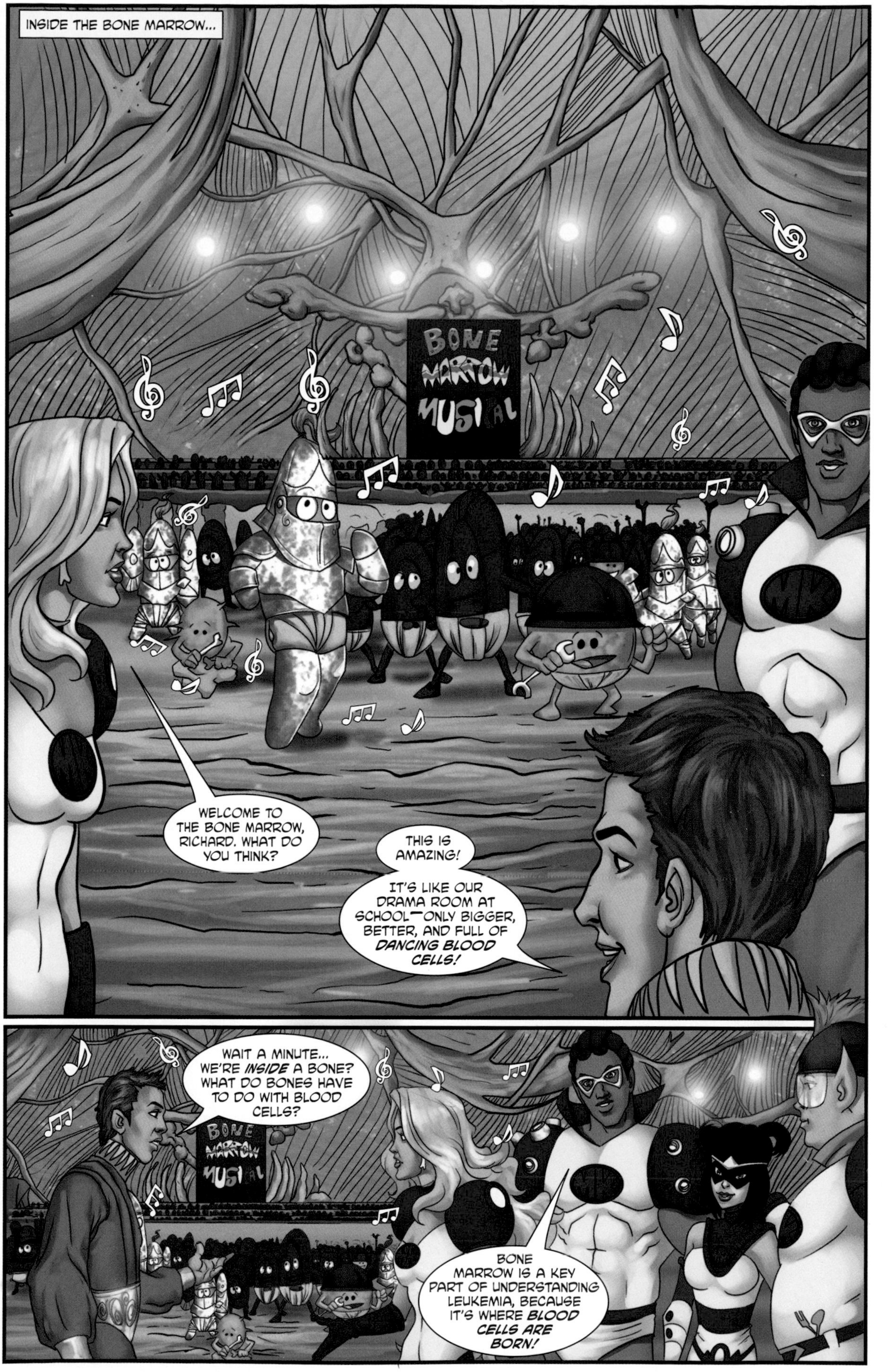
INSIDE THE BONE MARROW...
BONE MARROW MUSICAL
WELCOME TO THE BONE MARROW, RICHARD. WHAT DO YOU THINK?
THIS IS AMAZING!
IT'S LIKE OUR DRAMA ROOM AT SCHOOL—ONLY BIGGER, BETTER, AND FULL OF *DANCING BLOOD CELLS!*
WAIT A MINUTE... WE'RE *INSIDE* A BONE? WHAT DO BONES HAVE TO DO WITH BLOOD CELLS?
BONE MARROW IS A KEY PART OF UNDERSTANDING LEUKEMIA, BECAUSE IT'S WHERE *BLOOD CELLS ARE BORN!*

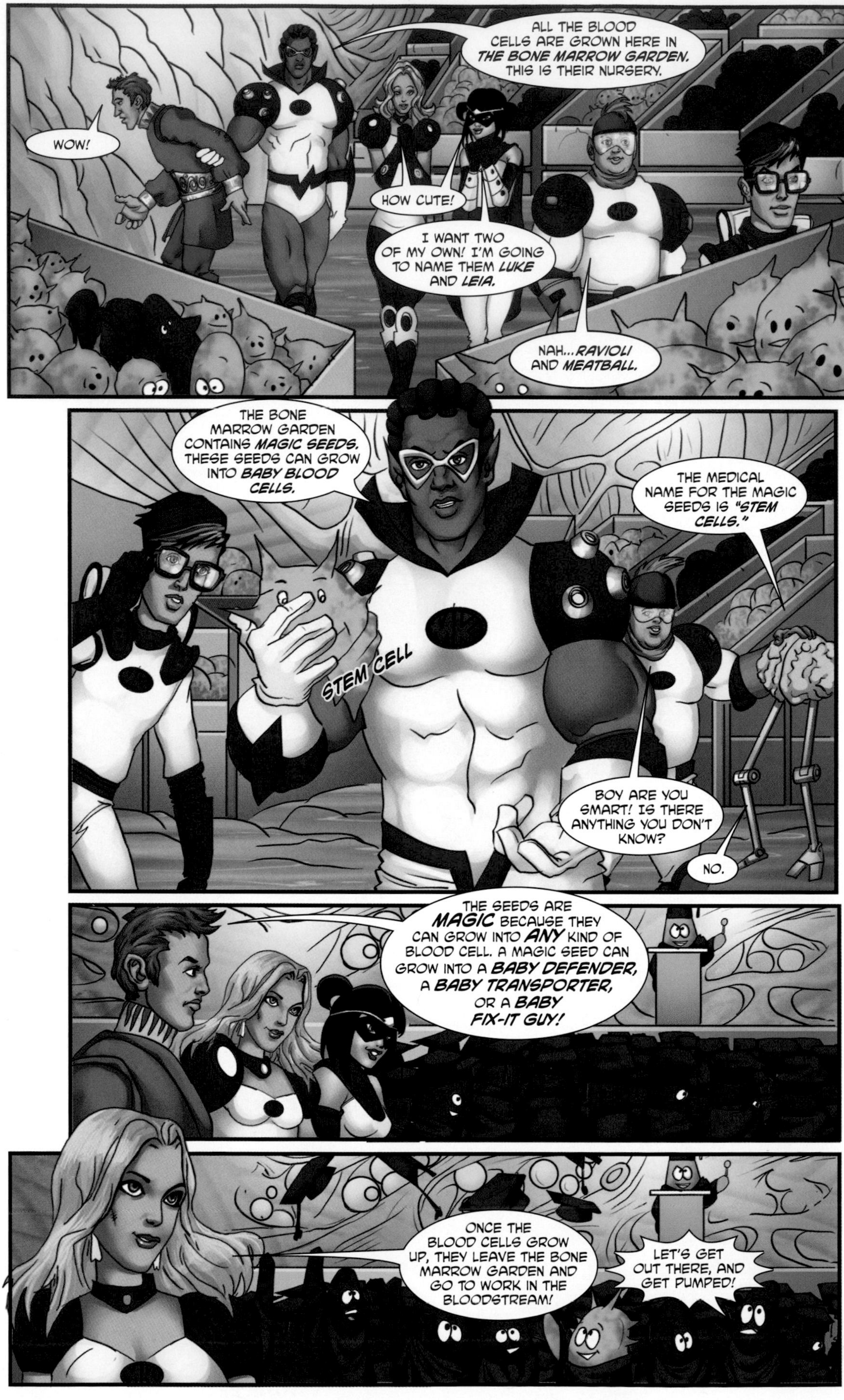
ALL THE BLOOD CELLS ARE GROWN HERE IN THE BONE MARROW GARDEN. THIS IS THEIR NURSERY.
WOW!
HOW CUTE!
I WANT TWO OF MY OWN! I'M GOING TO NAME THEM LUKE AND LEIA.
NAH...RAVIOLI AND MEATBALL.
THE BONE MARROW GARDEN CONTAINS MAGIC SEEDS. THESE SEEDS CAN GROW INTO BABY BLOOD CELLS.
STEM CELL
THE MEDICAL NAME FOR THE MAGIC SEEDS IS "STEM CELLS."
BOY ARE YOU SMART! IS THERE ANYTHING YOU DON'T KNOW?
NO.
THE SEEDS ARE MAGIC BECAUSE THEY CAN GROW INTO ANY KIND OF BLOOD CELL. A MAGIC SEED CAN GROW INTO A BABY DEFENDER, A BABY TRANSPORTER, OR A BABY FIX-IT GUY!
ONCE THE BLOOD CELLS GROW UP, THEY LEAVE THE BONE MARROW GARDEN AND GO TO WORK IN THE BLOODSTREAM!
LET'S GET OUT THERE, AND GET PUMPED!

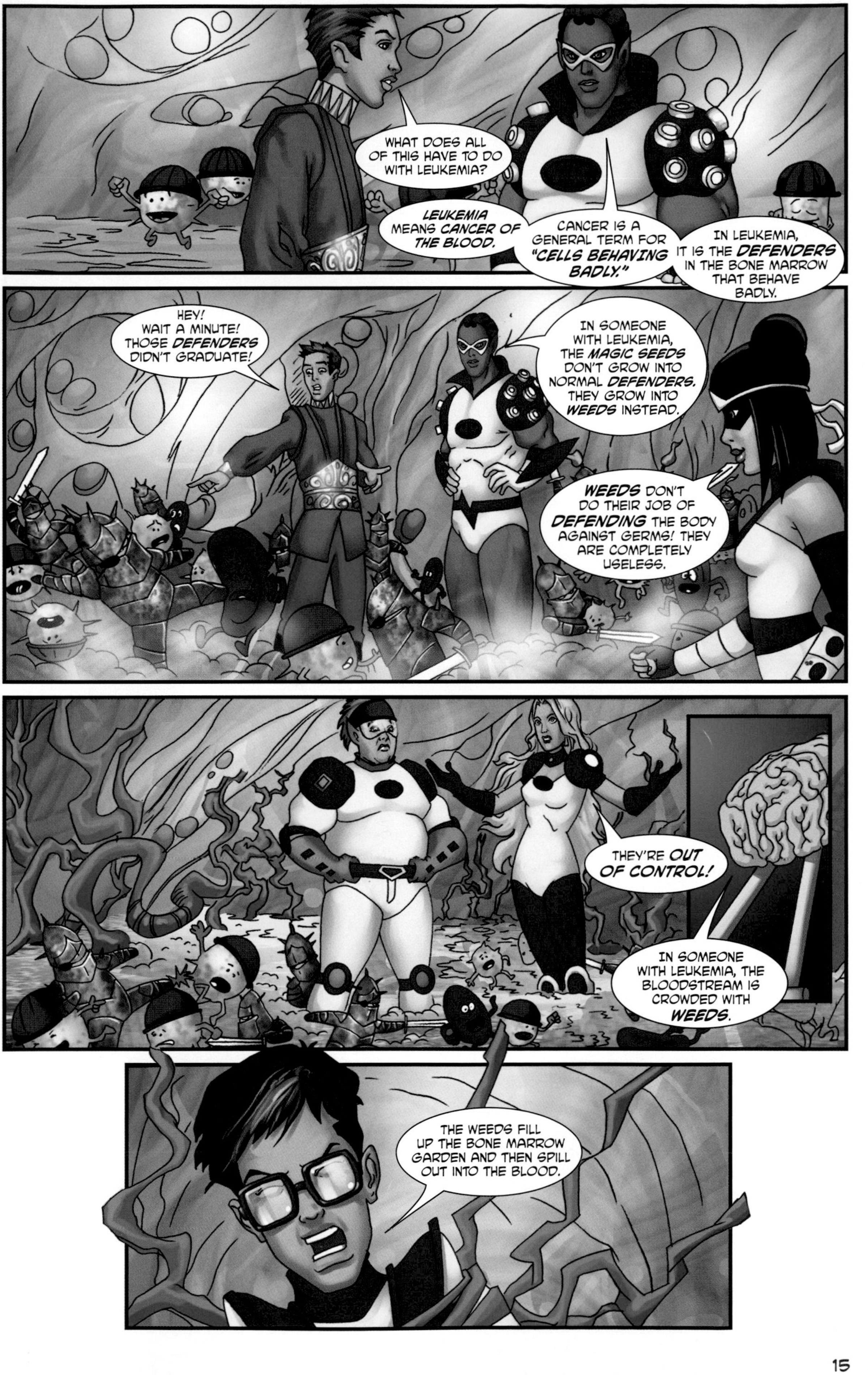
WHAT DOES ALL OF THIS HAVE TO DO WITH LEUKEMIA?
LEUKEMIA MEANS CANCER OF THE BLOOD.
CANCER IS A GENERAL TERM FOR "CELLS BEHAVING BADLY."
IN LEUKEMIA, IT IS THE DEFENDERS IN THE BONE MARROW THAT BEHAVE BADLY.
HEY! WAIT A MINUTE! THOSE DEFENDERS DIDN'T GRADUATE!
IN SOMEONE WITH LEUKEMIA, THE MAGIC SEEDS DON'T GROW INTO NORMAL DEFENDERS. THEY GROW INTO WEEDS INSTEAD.
WEEDS DON'T DO THEIR JOB OF DEFENDING THE BODY AGAINST GERMS! THEY ARE COMPLETELY USELESS.
THEY'RE OUT OF CONTROL!
IN SOMEONE WITH LEUKEMIA, THE BLOODSTREAM IS CROWDED WITH WEEDS.
THE WEEDS FILL UP THE BONE MARROW GARDEN AND THEN SPILL OUT INTO THE BLOOD.

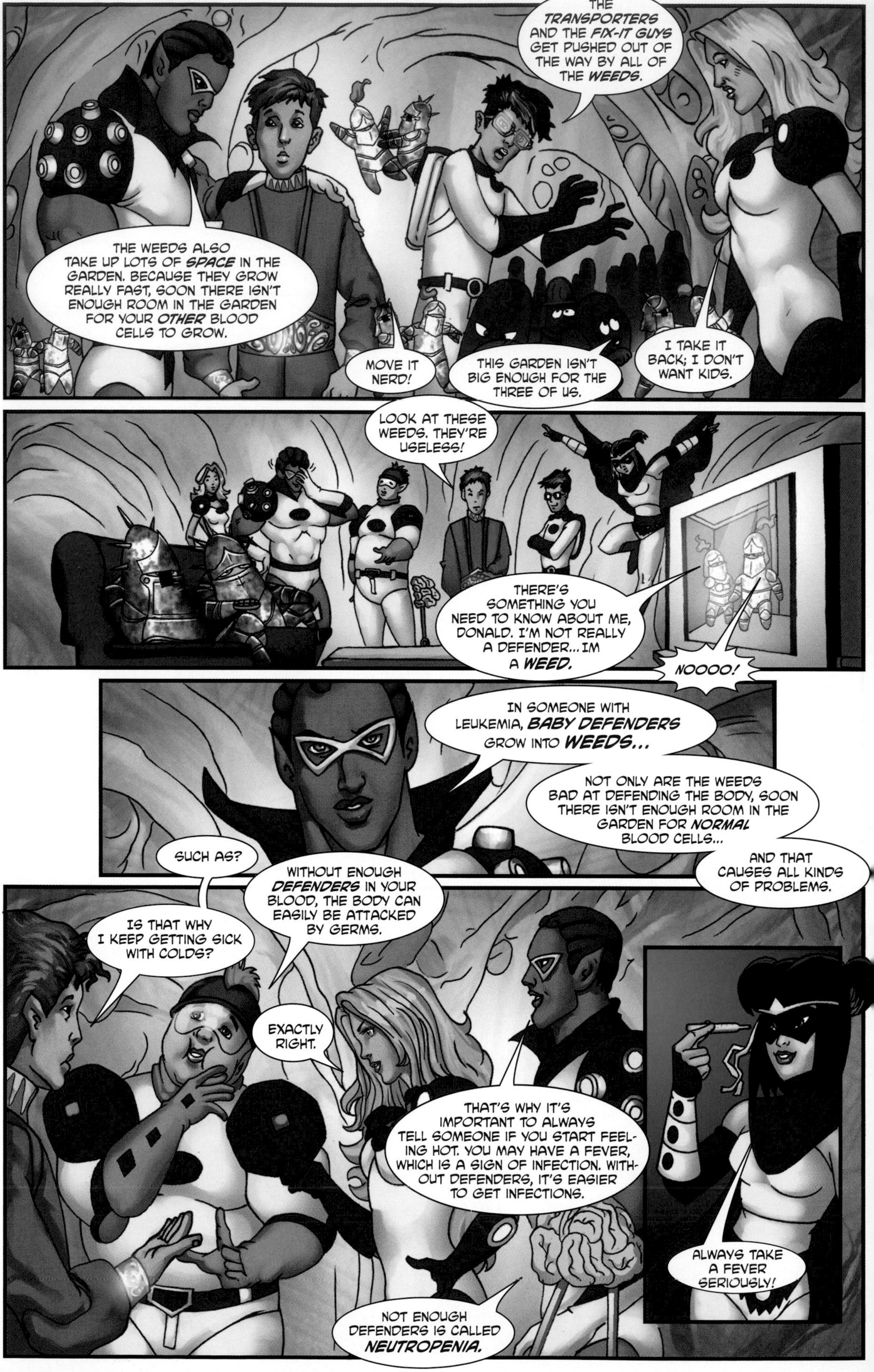
THE TRANSPORTERS AND THE FIX-IT GUYS GET PUSHED OUT OF THE WAY BY ALL OF THE WEEDS.
THE WEEDS ALSO TAKE UP LOTS OF SPACE IN THE GARDEN. BECAUSE THEY GROW REALLY FAST, SOON THERE ISN'T ENOUGH ROOM IN THE GARDEN FOR YOUR OTHER BLOOD CELLS TO GROW.
MOVE IT NERD!
THIS GARDEN ISN'T BIG ENOUGH FOR THE THREE OF US.
I TAKE IT BACK; I DON'T WANT KIDS.
LOOK AT THESE WEEDS. THEY'RE USELESS!
THERE'S SOMETHING YOU NEED TO KNOW ABOUT ME, DONALD. I'M NOT REALLY A DEFENDER...IM A WEED.
NOOOO!
IN SOMEONE WITH LEUKEMIA, BABY DEFENDERS GROW INTO WEEDS...
NOT ONLY ARE THE WEEDS BAD AT DEFENDING THE BODY, SOON THERE ISN'T ENOUGH ROOM IN THE GARDEN FOR NORMAL BLOOD CELLS...
AND THAT CAUSES ALL KINDS OF PROBLEMS.
SUCH AS?
WITHOUT ENOUGH DEFENDERS IN YOUR BLOOD, THE BODY CAN EASILY BE ATTACKED BY GERMS.
IS THAT WHY I KEEP GETTING SICK WITH COLDS?
EXACTLY RIGHT.
THAT'S WHY IT'S IMPORTANT TO ALWAYS TELL SOMEONE IF YOU START FEELING HOT. YOU MAY HAVE A FEVER, WHICH IS A SIGN OF INFECTION. WITHOUT DEFENDERS, IT'S EASIER TO GET INFECTIONS.
ALWAYS TAKE A FEVER SERIOUSLY!
NOT ENOUGH DEFENDERS IS CALLED NEUTROPENIA.

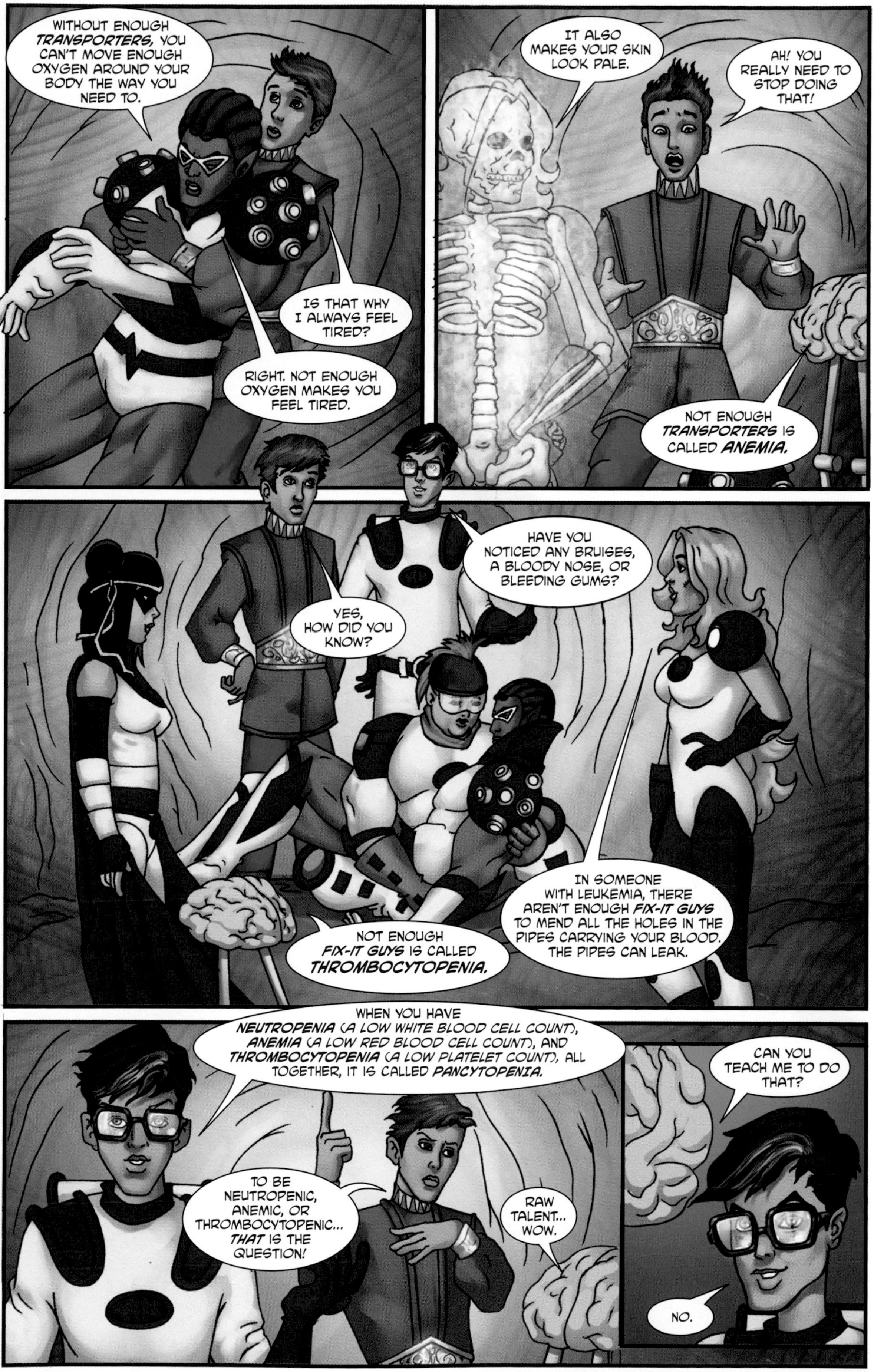
WITHOUT ENOUGH *TRANSPORTERS,* YOU CAN'T MOVE ENOUGH OXYGEN AROUND YOUR BODY THE WAY YOU NEED TO.
IS THAT WHY I ALWAYS FEEL TIRED?
RIGHT. NOT ENOUGH OXYGEN MAKES YOU FEEL TIRED.
IT ALSO MAKES YOUR SKIN LOOK PALE.
AH! YOU REALLY NEED TO STOP DOING THAT!
NOT ENOUGH *TRANSPORTERS* IS CALLED ***ANEMIA.***
HAVE YOU NOTICED ANY BRUISES, A BLOODY NOSE, OR BLEEDING GUMS?
YES, HOW DID YOU KNOW?
IN SOMEONE WITH LEUKEMIA, THERE AREN'T ENOUGH *FIX-IT GUYS* TO MEND ALL THE HOLES IN THE PIPES CARRYING YOUR BLOOD. THE PIPES CAN LEAK.
NOT ENOUGH *FIX-IT GUYS* IS CALLED ***THROMBOCYTOPENIA.***
WHEN YOU HAVE *NEUTROPENIA (A LOW WHITE BLOOD CELL COUNT), ANEMIA (A LOW RED BLOOD CELL COUNT),* AND *THROMBOCYTOPENIA (A LOW PLATELET COUNT),* ALL TOGETHER, IT IS CALLED *PANCYTOPENIA.*
TO BE NEUTROPENIC, ANEMIC, OR THROMBOCYTOPENIC... *THAT* IS THE QUESTION!
RAW TALENT... WOW.
CAN YOU TEACH ME TO DO THAT?
NO.

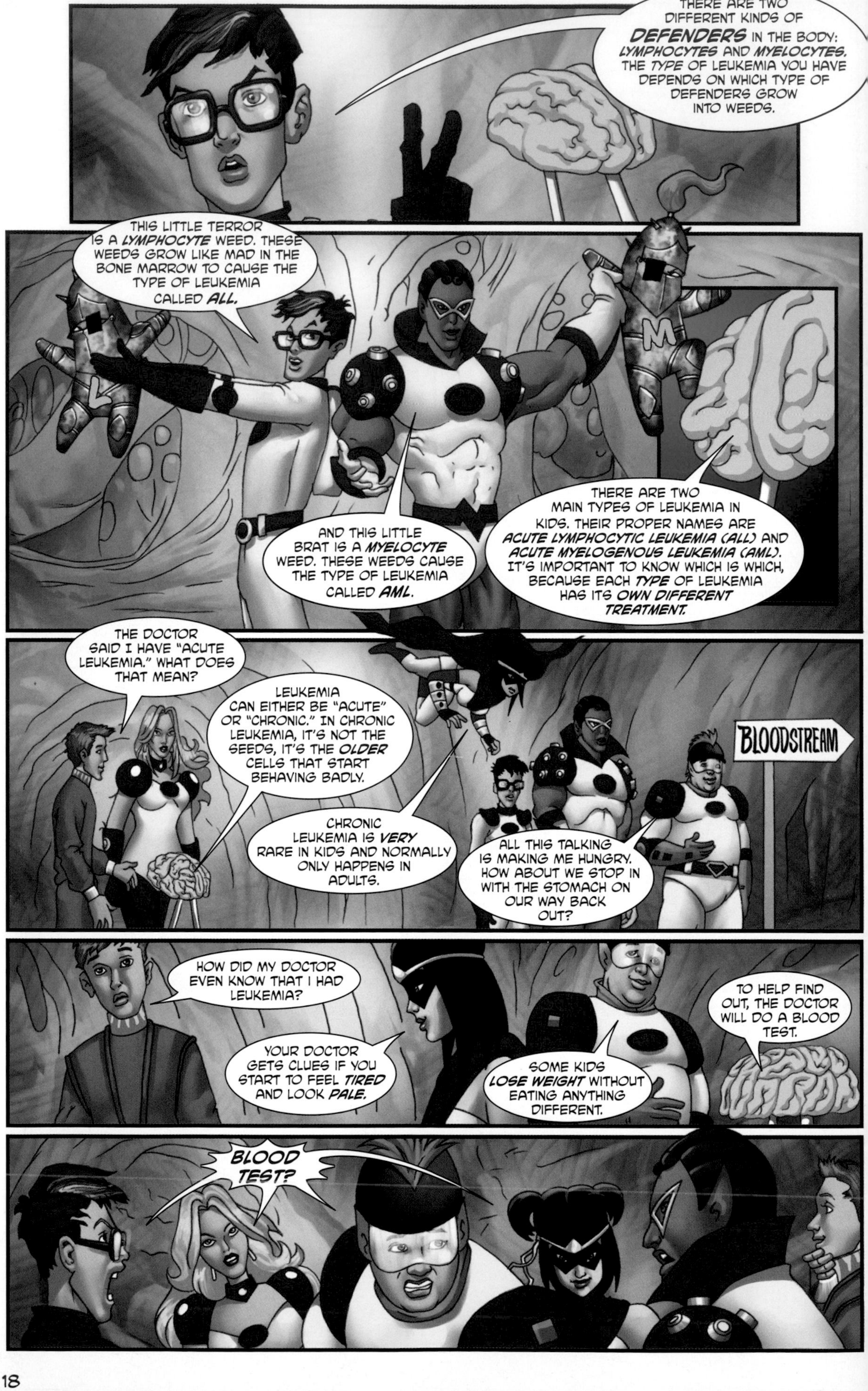
THERE ARE TWO DIFFERENT KINDS OF DEFENDERS IN THE BODY: LYMPHOCYTES AND MYELOCYTES. THE TYPE OF LEUKEMIA YOU HAVE DEPENDS ON WHICH TYPE OF DEFENDERS GROW INTO WEEDS.
THIS LITTLE TERROR IS A LYMPHOCYTE WEED. THESE WEEDS GROW LIKE MAD IN THE BONE MARROW TO CAUSE THE TYPE OF LEUKEMIA CALLED ALL.
AND THIS LITTLE BRAT IS A MYELOCYTE WEED. THESE WEEDS CAUSE THE TYPE OF LEUKEMIA CALLED AML.
THERE ARE TWO MAIN TYPES OF LEUKEMIA IN KIDS. THEIR PROPER NAMES ARE ACUTE LYMPHOCYTIC LEUKEMIA (ALL) AND ACUTE MYELOGENOUS LEUKEMIA (AML). IT'S IMPORTANT TO KNOW WHICH IS WHICH, BECAUSE EACH TYPE OF LEUKEMIA HAS ITS OWN DIFFERENT TREATMENT.
THE DOCTOR SAID I HAVE "ACUTE LEUKEMIA." WHAT DOES THAT MEAN?
LEUKEMIA CAN EITHER BE "ACUTE" OR "CHRONIC." IN CHRONIC LEUKEMIA, IT'S NOT THE SEEDS, IT'S THE OLDER CELLS THAT START BEHAVING BADLY.
CHRONIC LEUKEMIA IS VERY RARE IN KIDS AND NORMALLY ONLY HAPPENS IN ADULTS.
BLOODSTREAM
ALL THIS TALKING IS MAKING ME HUNGRY. HOW ABOUT WE STOP IN WITH THE STOMACH ON OUR WAY BACK OUT?
HOW DID MY DOCTOR EVEN KNOW THAT I HAD LEUKEMIA?
YOUR DOCTOR GETS CLUES IF YOU START TO FEEL TIRED AND LOOK PALE.
SOME KIDS LOSE WEIGHT WITHOUT EATING ANYTHING DIFFERENT.
TO HELP FIND OUT, THE DOCTOR WILL DO A BLOOD TEST.
BLOOD TEST?

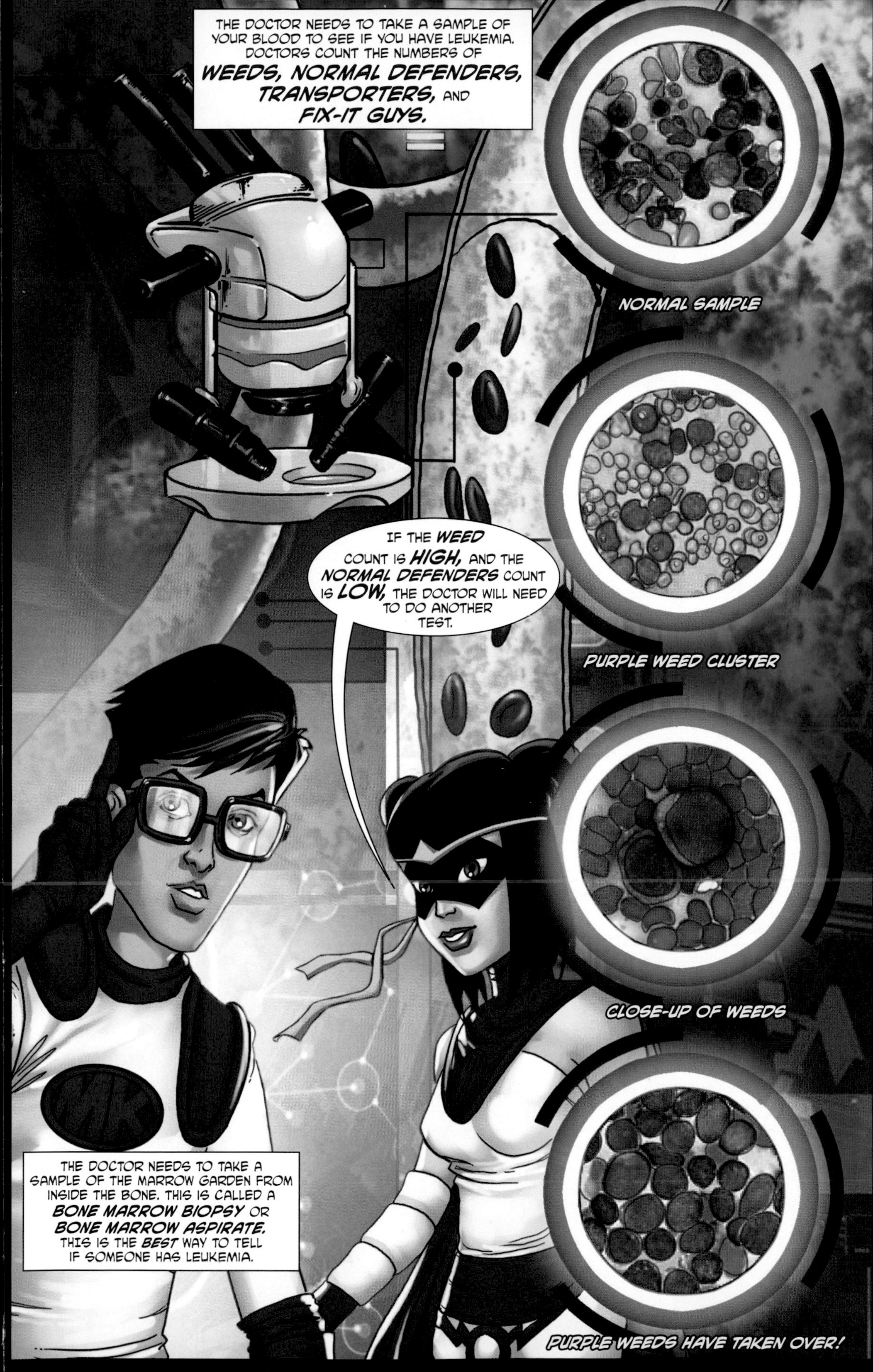
THE DOCTOR NEEDS TO TAKE A SAMPLE OF YOUR BLOOD TO SEE IF YOU HAVE LEUKEMIA. DOCTORS COUNT THE NUMBERS OF ***WEEDS, NORMAL DEFENDERS, TRANSPORTERS,*** AND ***FIX-IT GUYS.***
NORMAL SAMPLE
IF THE ***WEED*** COUNT IS ***HIGH,*** AND THE ***NORMAL DEFENDERS*** COUNT IS ***LOW,*** THE DOCTOR WILL NEED TO DO ANOTHER TEST.
PURPLE WEED CLUSTER
CLOSE-UP OF WEEDS
THE DOCTOR NEEDS TO TAKE A SAMPLE OF THE MARROW GARDEN FROM INSIDE THE BONE. THIS IS CALLED A ***BONE MARROW BIOPSY*** OR ***BONE MARROW ASPIRATE.*** THIS IS THE ***BEST*** WAY TO TELL IF SOMEONE HAS LEUKEMIA.
PURPLE WEEDS HAVE TAKEN OVER!

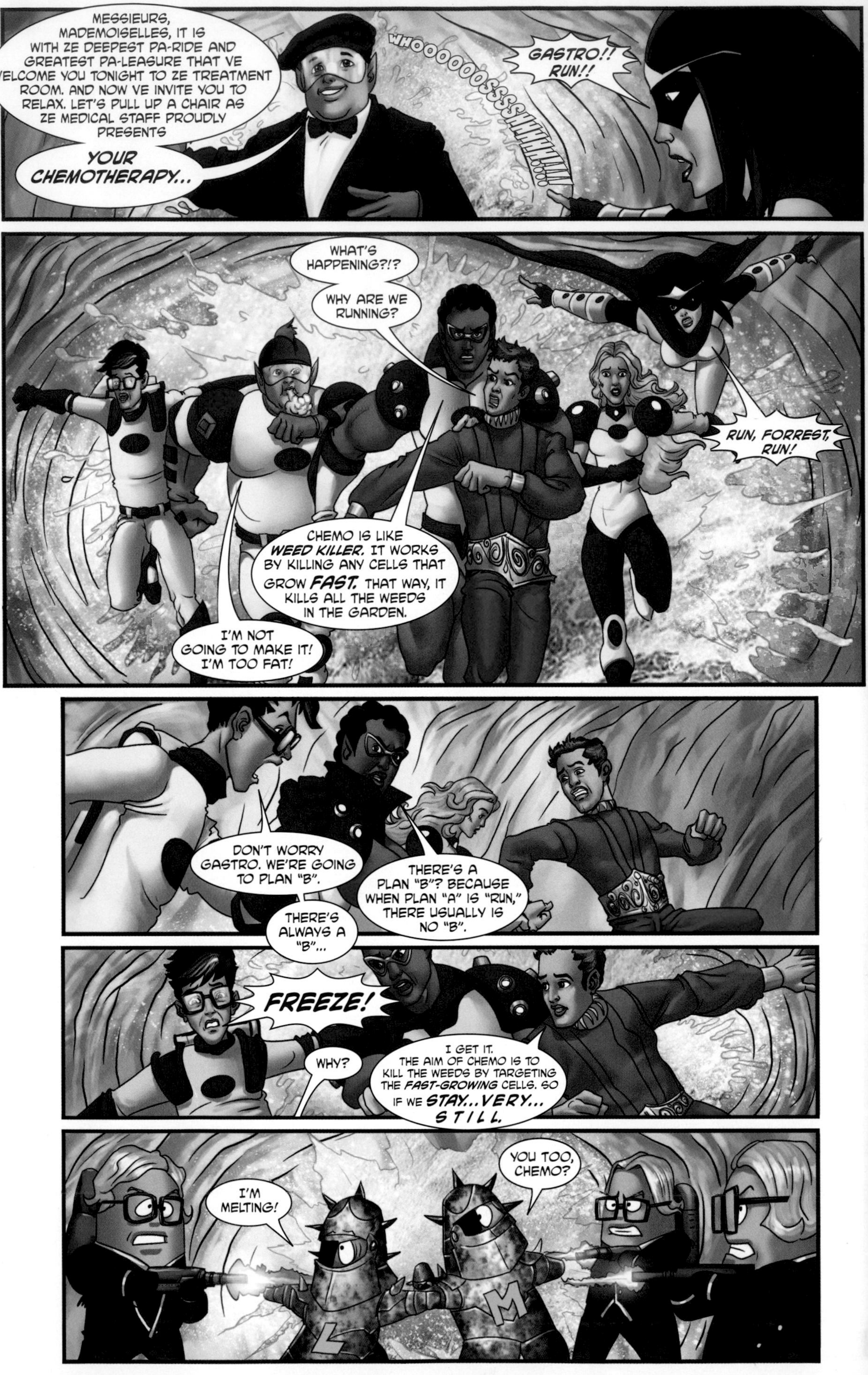

MESSIEURS, MADEMOISELLES, IT IS WITH ZE DEEPEST PA-RIDE AND GREATEST PA-LEASURE THAT VE VELCOME YOU TONIGHT TO ZE TREATMENT ROOM. AND NOW VE INVITE YOU TO RELAX. LET'S PULL UP A CHAIR AS ZE MEDICAL STAFF PROUDLY PRESENTS
YOUR CHEMOTHERAPY...
WHOOOOOOOSSSSHHHHH!!!!!
GASTRO!! RUN!!
WHAT'S HAPPENING?!?
WHY ARE WE RUNNING?
RUN, FORREST, RUN!
CHEMO IS LIKE WEED KILLER. IT WORKS BY KILLING ANY CELLS THAT GROW FAST. THAT WAY, IT KILLS ALL THE WEEDS IN THE GARDEN.
I'M NOT GOING TO MAKE IT! I'M TOO FAT!
DON'T WORRY GASTRO. WE'RE GOING TO PLAN "B".
THERE'S A PLAN "B"? BECAUSE WHEN PLAN "A" IS "RUN," THERE USUALLY IS NO "B".
THERE'S ALWAYS A "B"...
FREEZE!
WHY?
I GET IT. THE AIM OF CHEMO IS TO KILL THE WEEDS BY TARGETING THE FAST-GROWING CELLS. SO IF WE STAY...VERY... STILL.
I'M MELTING!
YOU TOO, CHEMO?

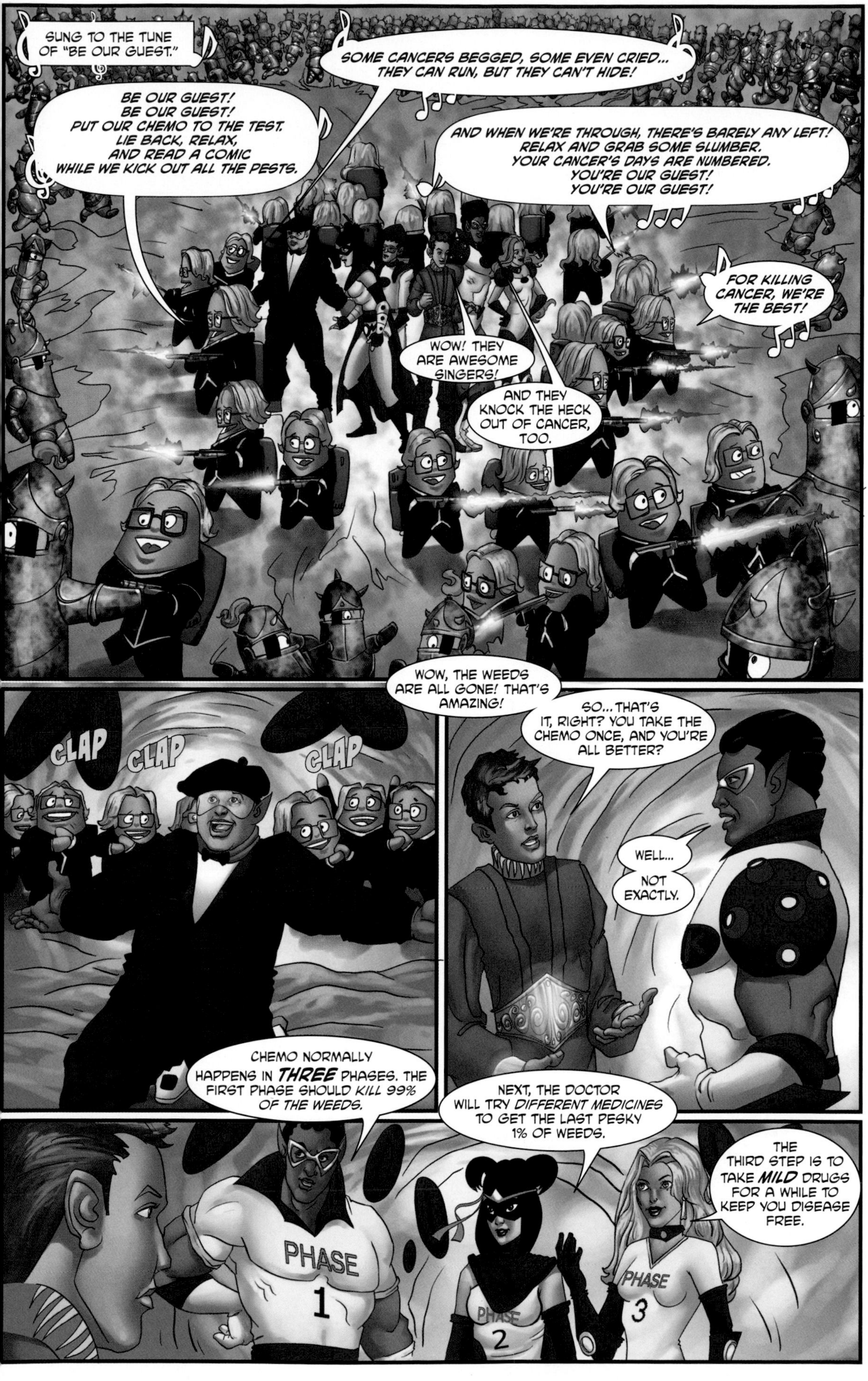
SUNG TO THE TUNE OF "BE OUR GUEST."
BE OUR GUEST! BE OUR GUEST! PUT OUR CHEMO TO THE TEST. LIE BACK, RELAX, AND READ A COMIC WHILE WE KICK OUT ALL THE PESTS.
SOME CANCERS BEGGED, SOME EVEN CRIED... THEY CAN RUN, BUT THEY CAN'T HIDE!
AND WHEN WE'RE THROUGH, THERE'S BARELY ANY LEFT! RELAX AND GRAB SOME SLUMBER. YOUR CANCER'S DAYS ARE NUMBERED. YOU'RE OUR GUEST! YOU'RE OUR GUEST!
FOR KILLING CANCER, WE'RE THE BEST!
WOW! THEY ARE AWESOME SINGERS!
AND THEY KNOCK THE HECK OUT OF CANCER, TOO.
CLAP
CLAP
CLAP
WOW, THE WEEDS ARE ALL GONE! THAT'S AMAZING!
SO... THAT'S IT, RIGHT? YOU TAKE THE CHEMO ONCE, AND YOU'RE ALL BETTER?
WELL...
NOT EXACTLY.
CHEMO NORMALLY HAPPENS IN THREE PHASES. THE FIRST PHASE SHOULD KILL 99% OF THE WEEDS.
NEXT, THE DOCTOR WILL TRY DIFFERENT MEDICINES TO GET THE LAST PESKY 1% OF WEEDS.
THE THIRD STEP IS TO TAKE MILD DRUGS FOR A WHILE TO KEEP YOU DISEASE FREE.
PHASE 1
PHASE 2
PHASE 3

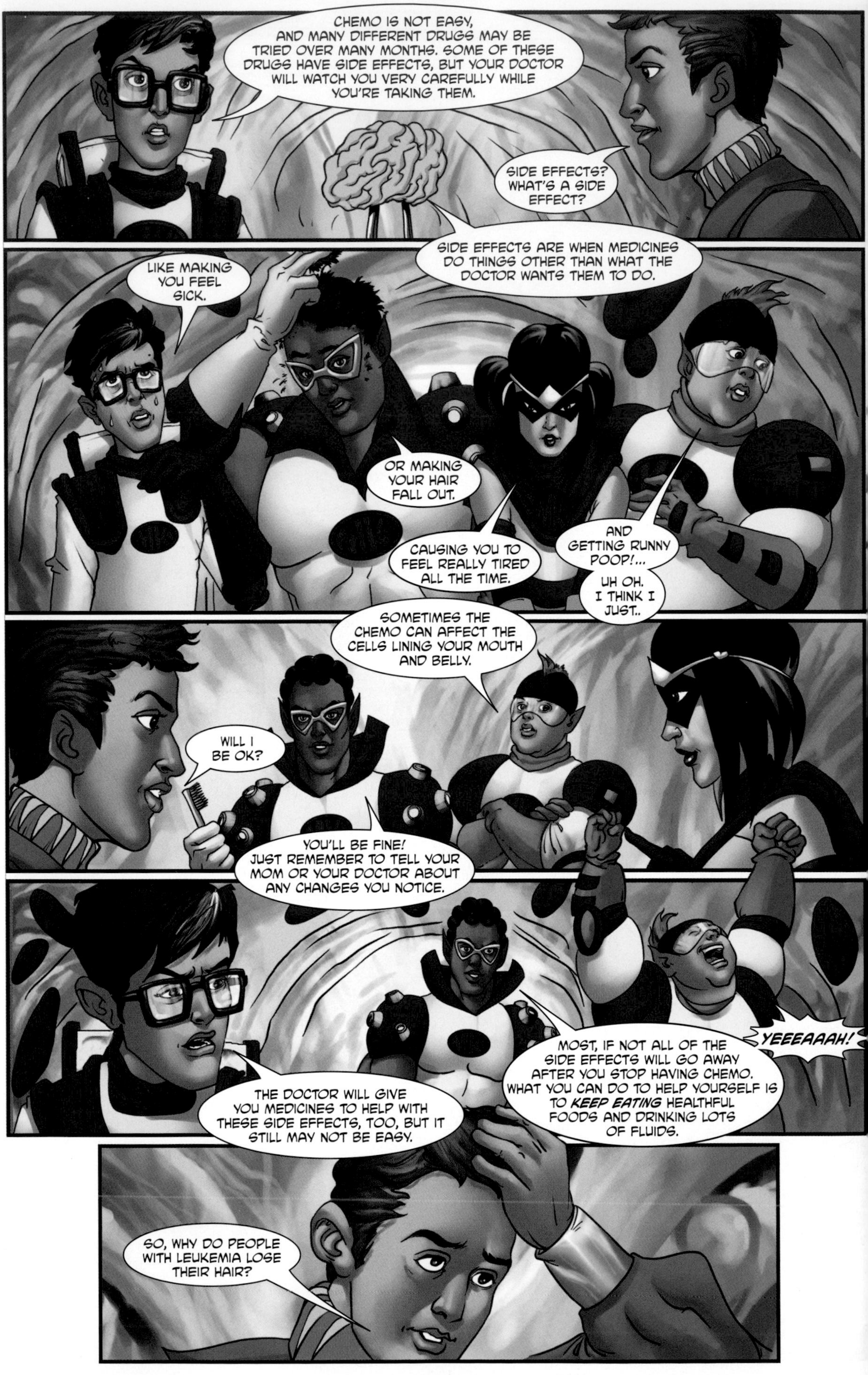

CHEMO IS NOT EASY, AND MANY DIFFERENT DRUGS MAY BE TRIED OVER MANY MONTHS. SOME OF THESE DRUGS HAVE SIDE EFFECTS, BUT YOUR DOCTOR WILL WATCH YOU VERY CAREFULLY WHILE YOU'RE TAKING THEM.
SIDE EFFECTS? WHAT'S A SIDE EFFECT?
SIDE EFFECTS ARE WHEN MEDICINES DO THINGS OTHER THAN WHAT THE DOCTOR WANTS THEM TO DO.
LIKE MAKING YOU FEEL SICK.
OR MAKING YOUR HAIR FALL OUT.
CAUSING YOU TO FEEL REALLY TIRED ALL THE TIME.
AND GETTING RUNNY POOP!...
UH OH. I THINK I JUST..
SOMETIMES THE CHEMO CAN AFFECT THE CELLS LINING YOUR MOUTH AND BELLY.
WILL I BE OK?
YOU'LL BE FINE! JUST REMEMBER TO TELL YOUR MOM OR YOUR DOCTOR ABOUT ANY CHANGES YOU NOTICE.
YEEEAAAH!
THE DOCTOR WILL GIVE YOU MEDICINES TO HELP WITH THESE SIDE EFFECTS, TOO, BUT IT STILL MAY NOT BE EASY.
MOST, IF NOT ALL OF THE SIDE EFFECTS WILL GO AWAY AFTER YOU STOP HAVING CHEMO. WHAT YOU CAN DO TO HELP YOURSELF IS TO KEEP EATING HEALTHFUL FOODS AND DRINKING LOTS OF FLUIDS.
SO, WHY DO PEOPLE WITH LEUKEMIA LOSE THEIR HAIR?

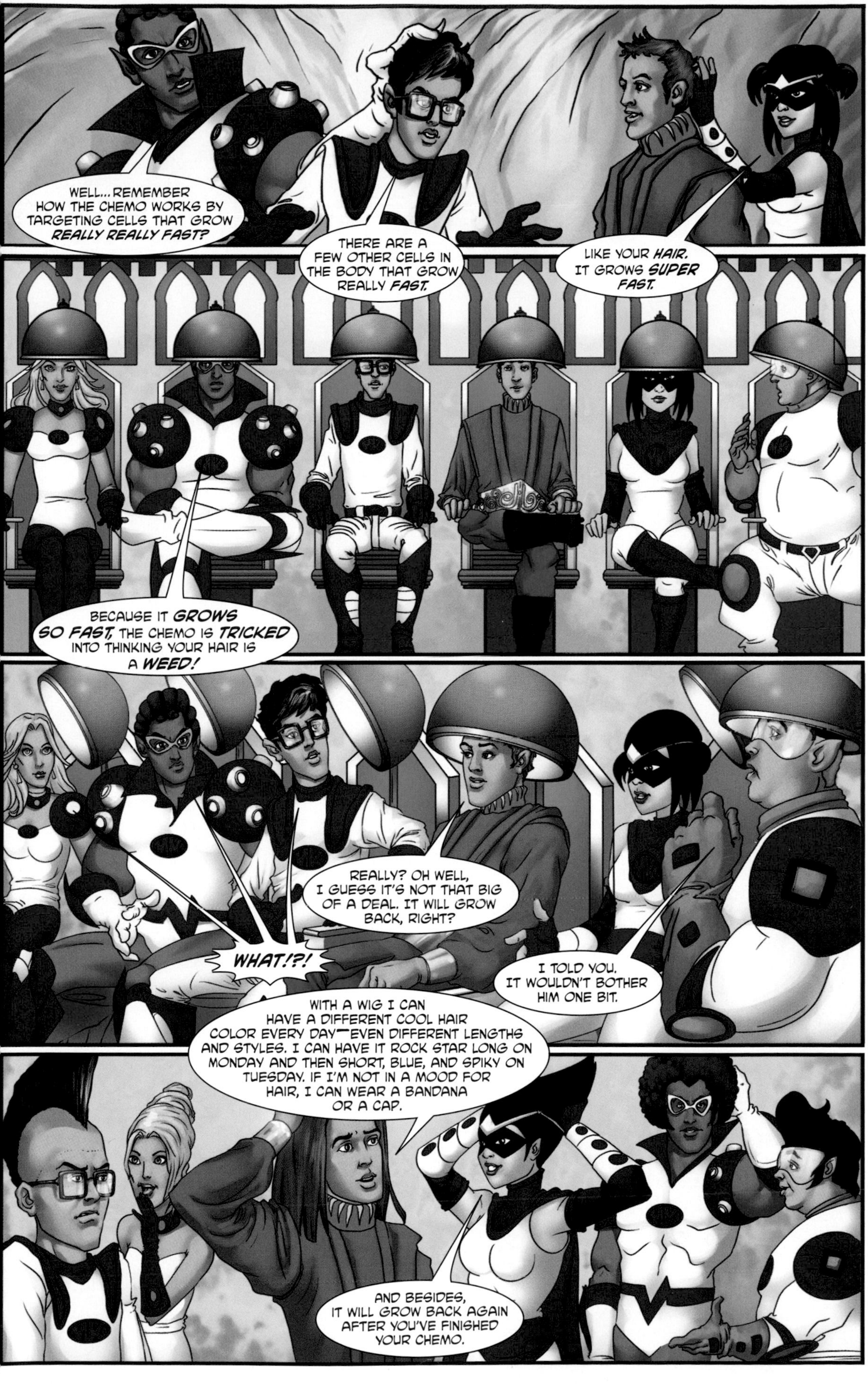
WELL... REMEMBER HOW THE CHEMO WORKS BY TARGETING CELLS THAT GROW REALLY REALLY FAST?
THERE ARE A FEW OTHER CELLS IN THE BODY THAT GROW REALLY FAST.
LIKE YOUR HAIR. IT GROWS SUPER FAST.
BECAUSE IT GROWS SO FAST, THE CHEMO IS TRICKED INTO THINKING YOUR HAIR IS A WEED!
REALLY? OH WELL, I GUESS IT'S NOT THAT BIG OF A DEAL. IT WILL GROW BACK, RIGHT?
WHAT!?!
I TOLD YOU. IT WOULDN'T BOTHER HIM ONE BIT.
WITH A WIG I CAN HAVE A DIFFERENT COOL HAIR COLOR EVERY DAY—EVEN DIFFERENT LENGTHS AND STYLES. I CAN HAVE IT ROCK STAR LONG ON MONDAY AND THEN SHORT, BLUE, AND SPIKY ON TUESDAY. IF I'M NOT IN A MOOD FOR HAIR, I CAN WEAR A BANDANA OR A CAP.
AND BESIDES, IT WILL GROW BACK AGAIN AFTER YOU'VE FINISHED YOUR CHEMO.

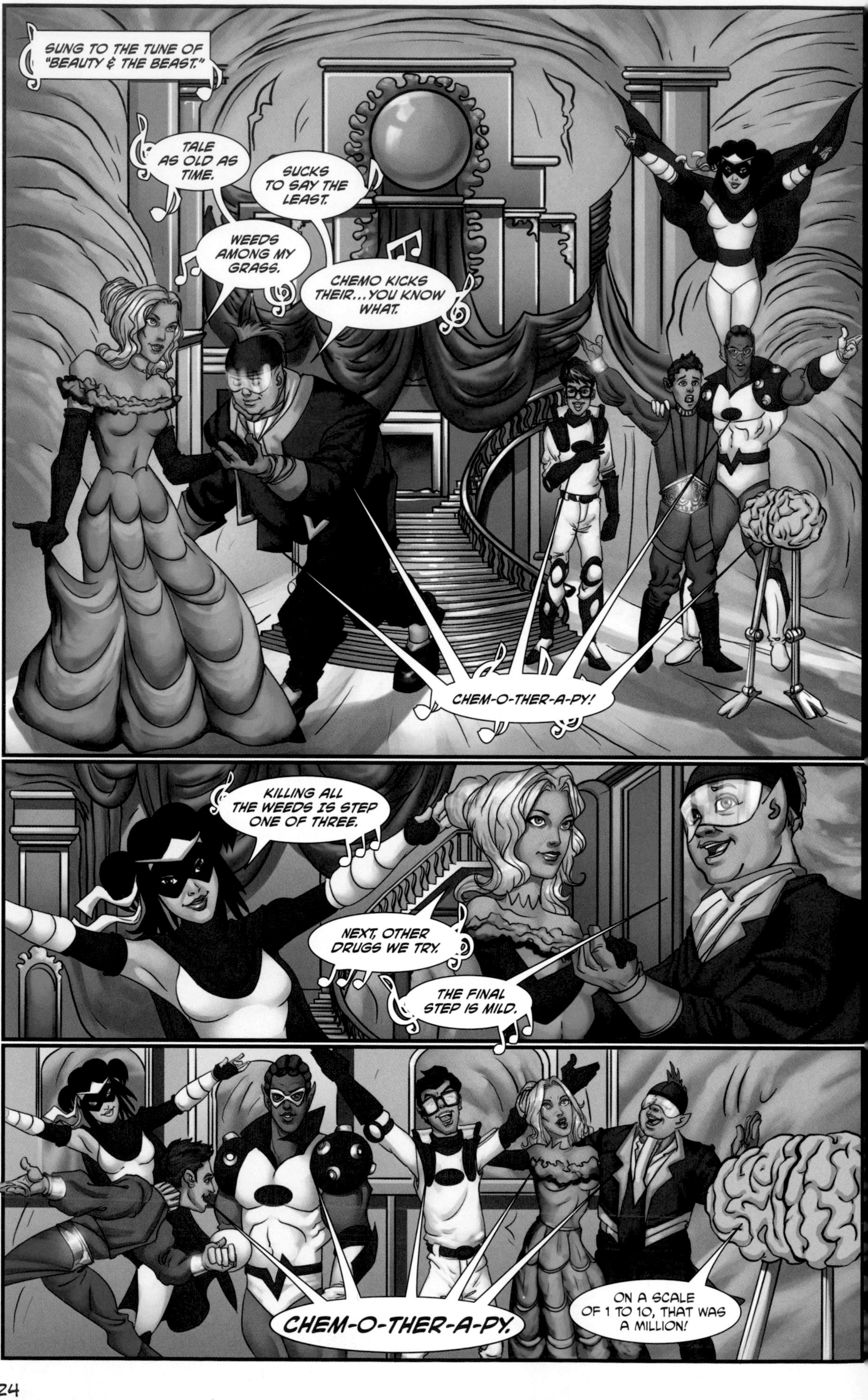
SUNG TO THE TUNE OF "BEAUTY & THE BEAST."
TALE AS OLD AS TIME.
SUCKS TO SAY THE LEAST.
WEEDS AMONG MY GRASS.
CHEMO KICKS THEIR...YOU KNOW WHAT.
CHEM-O-THER-A-PY!
KILLING ALL THE WEEDS IS STEP ONE OF THREE.
NEXT, OTHER DRUGS WE TRY.
THE FINAL STEP IS MILD.
CHEM-O-THER-A-PY.
ON A SCALE OF 1 TO 10, THAT WAS A MILLION!

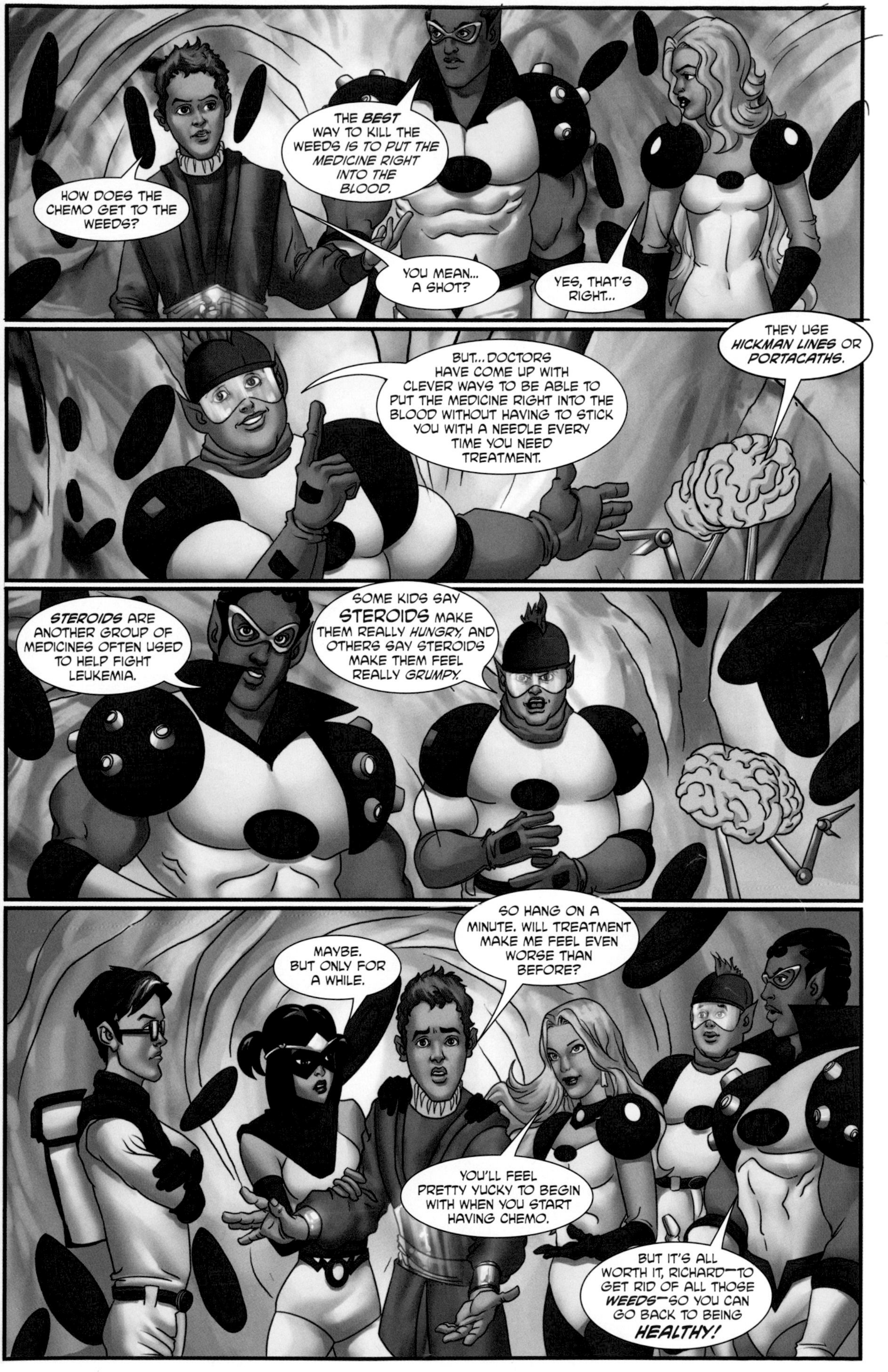

HOW DOES THE CHEMO GET TO THE WEEDS?
THE *BEST* WAY TO KILL THE WEEDS *IS TO PUT THE MEDICINE RIGHT INTO THE BLOOD.*
YOU MEAN... A SHOT?
YES, THAT'S RIGHT...
BUT... DOCTORS HAVE COME UP WITH CLEVER WAYS TO BE ABLE TO PUT THE MEDICINE RIGHT INTO THE BLOOD WITHOUT HAVING TO STICK YOU WITH A NEEDLE EVERY TIME YOU NEED TREATMENT.
THEY USE *HICKMAN LINES* OR *PORTACATHS*.
STEROIDS ARE ANOTHER GROUP OF MEDICINES OFTEN USED TO HELP FIGHT LEUKEMIA.
SOME KIDS SAY **STEROIDS** MAKE THEM REALLY *HUNGRY,* AND OTHERS SAY STEROIDS MAKE THEM FEEL REALLY *GRUMPY.*
MAYBE. BUT ONLY FOR A WHILE.
SO HANG ON A MINUTE. WILL TREATMENT MAKE ME FEEL EVEN WORSE THAN BEFORE?
YOU'LL FEEL PRETTY YUCKY TO BEGIN WITH WHEN YOU START HAVING CHEMO.
BUT IT'S ALL WORTH IT, RICHARD—TO GET RID OF ALL THOSE *WEEDS*—SO YOU CAN GO BACK TO BEING ***HEALTHY!***

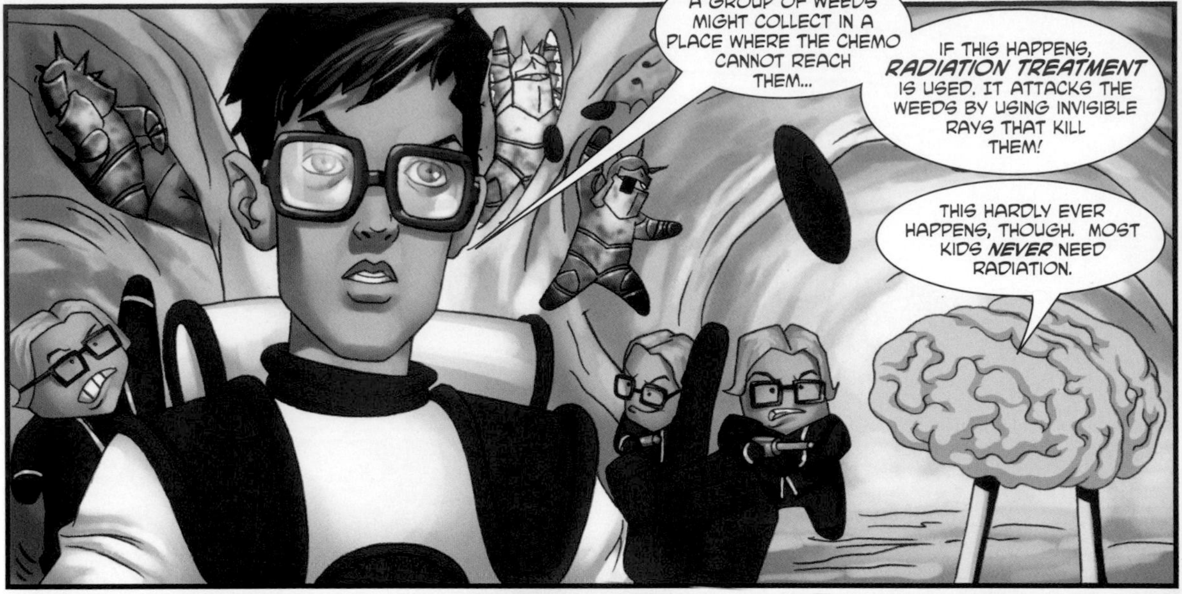
SOMETIMES, A GROUP OF WEEDS MIGHT COLLECT IN A PLACE WHERE THE CHEMO CANNOT REACH THEM...
IF THIS HAPPENS, ***RADIATION TREATMENT*** IS USED. IT ATTACKS THE WEEDS BY USING INVISIBLE RAYS THAT KILL THEM!
THIS HARDLY EVER HAPPENS, THOUGH. MOST KIDS ***NEVER*** NEED RADIATION.

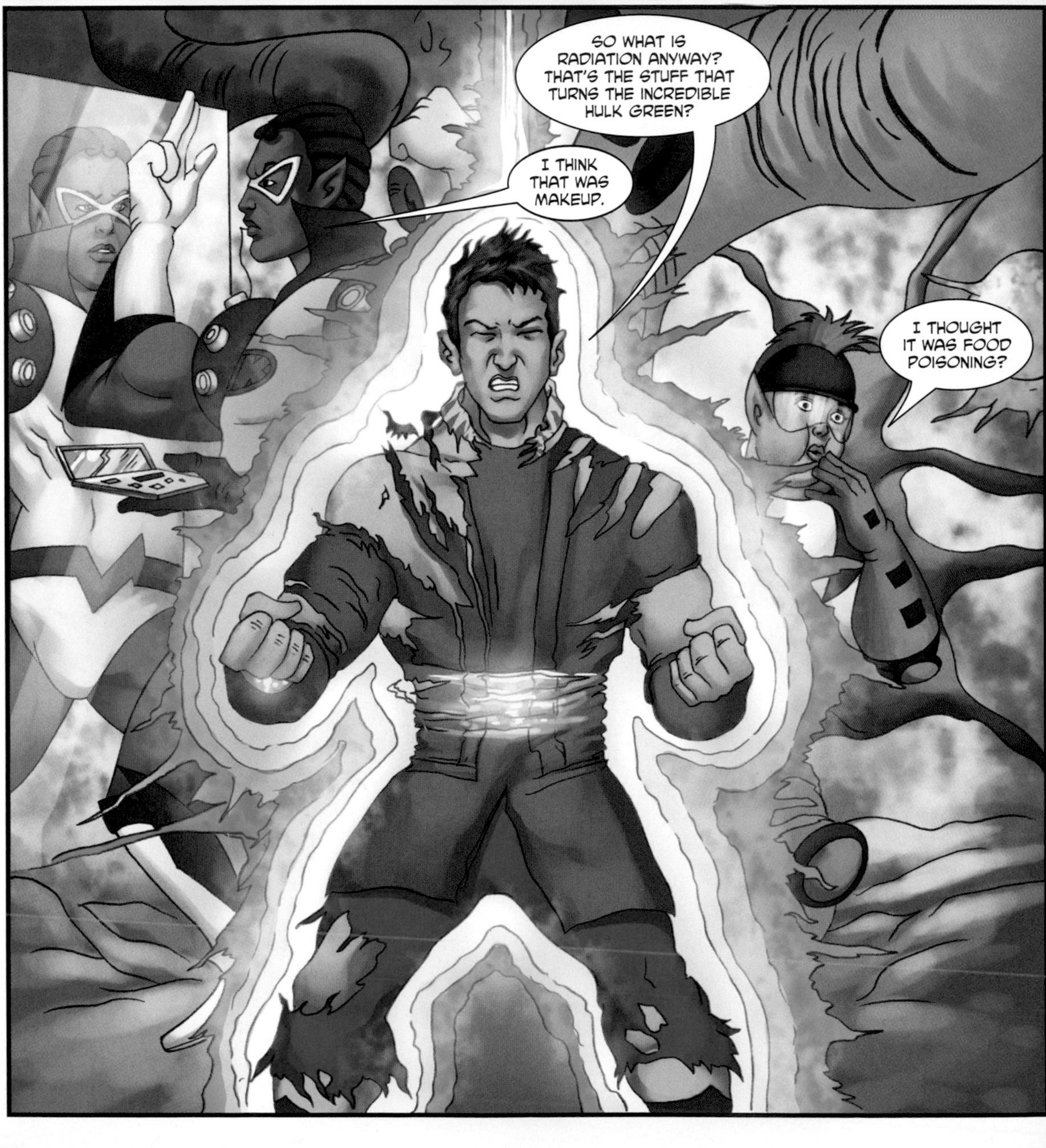
SO WHAT IS RADIATION ANYWAY? THAT'S THE STUFF THAT TURNS THE INCREDIBLE HULK GREEN?
I THINK THAT WAS MAKEUP.
I THOUGHT IT WAS FOOD POISONING?

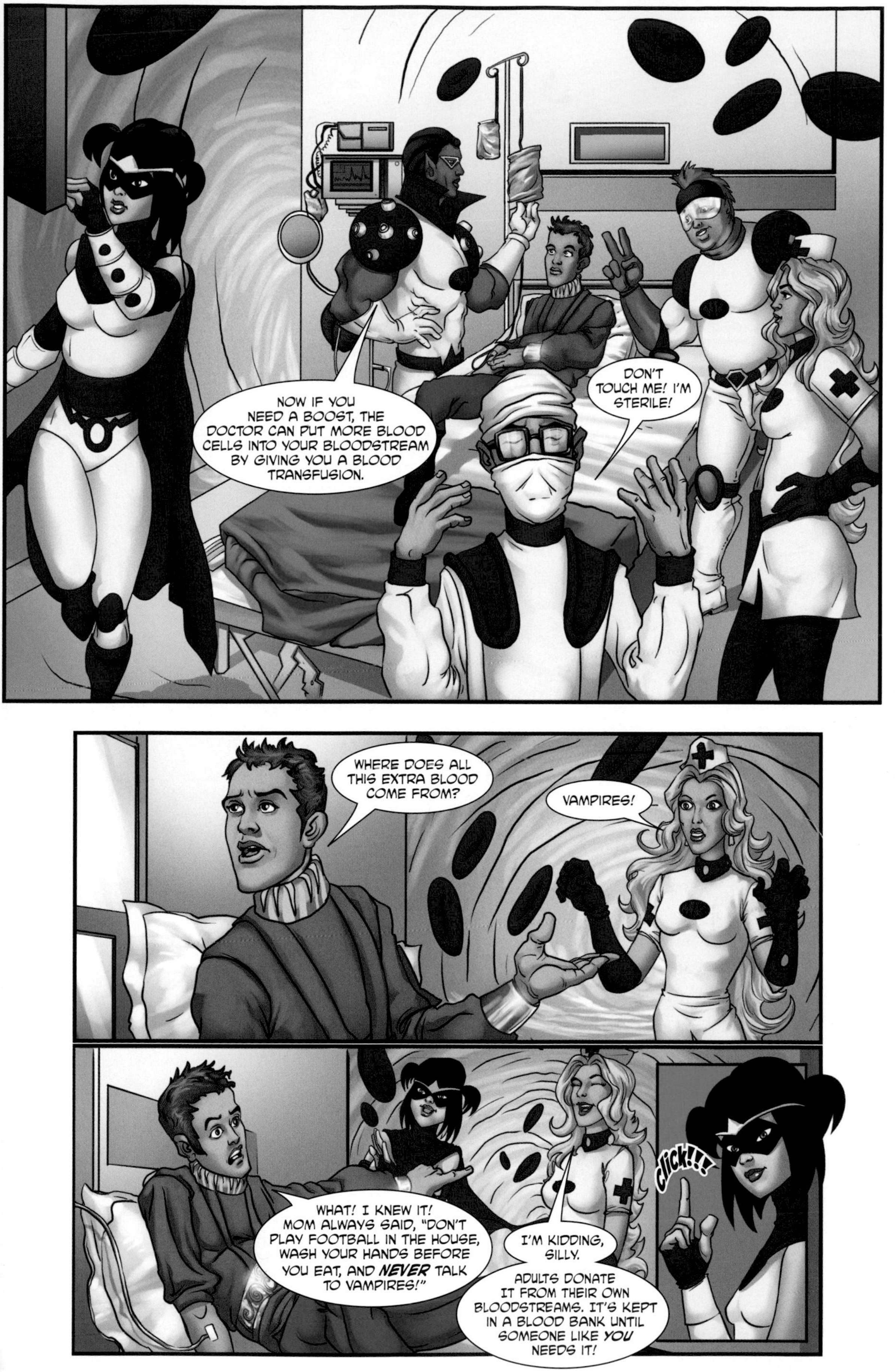
NOW IF YOU NEED A BOOST, THE DOCTOR CAN PUT MORE BLOOD CELLS INTO YOUR BLOODSTREAM BY GIVING YOU A BLOOD TRANSFUSION.
DON'T TOUCH ME! I'M STERILE!
WHERE DOES ALL THIS EXTRA BLOOD COME FROM?
VAMPIRES!
WHAT! I KNEW IT! MOM ALWAYS SAID, "DON'T PLAY FOOTBALL IN THE HOUSE, WASH YOUR HANDS BEFORE YOU EAT, AND ***NEVER*** TALK TO VAMPIRES!"
I'M KIDDING, SILLY.
ADULTS DONATE IT FROM THEIR OWN BLOODSTREAMS. IT'S KEPT IN A BLOOD BANK UNTIL SOMEONE LIKE ***YOU*** NEEDS IT!
click!!!

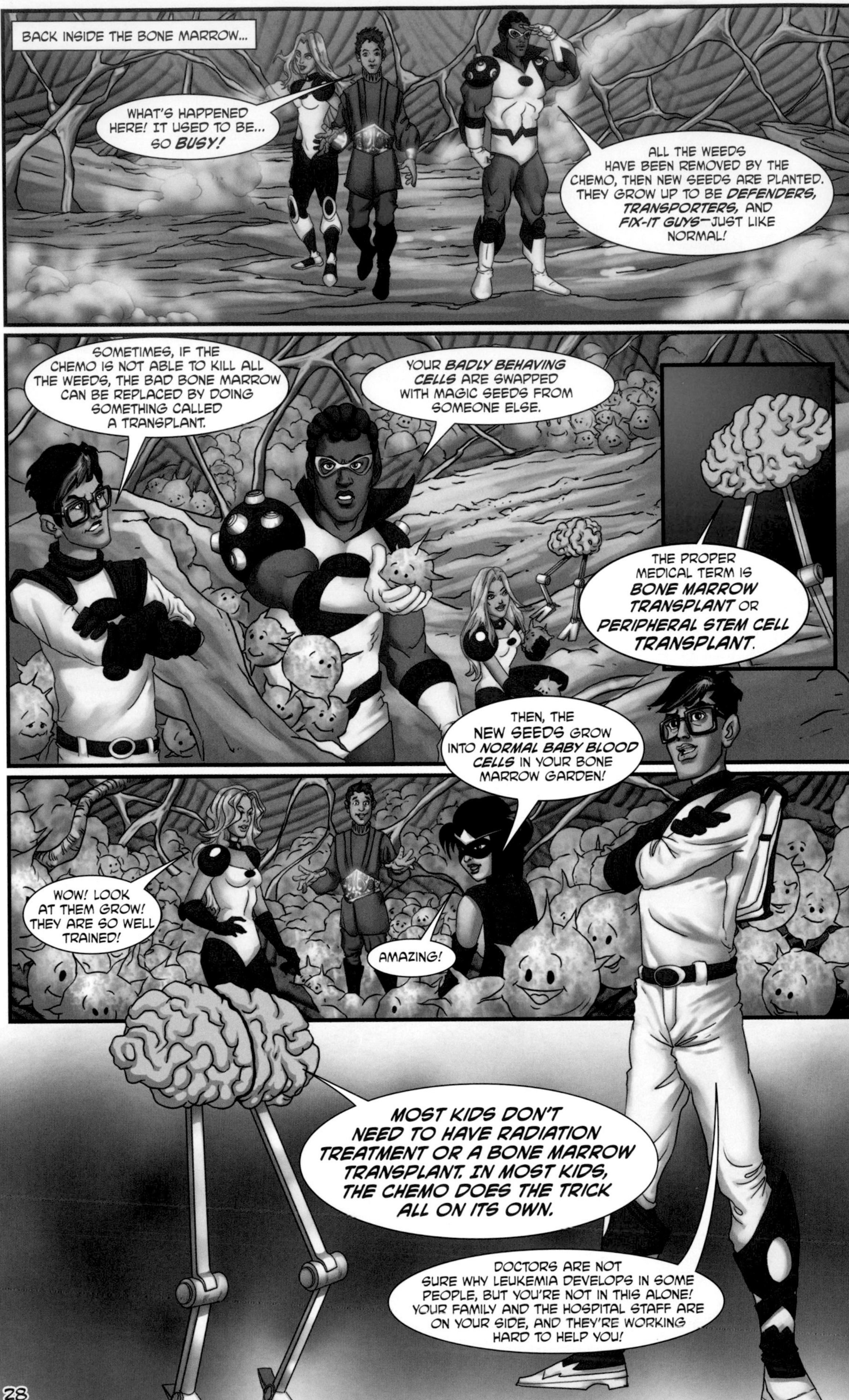
BACK INSIDE THE BONE MARROW...
WHAT'S HAPPENED HERE! IT USED TO BE... SO BUSY!
ALL THE WEEDS HAVE BEEN REMOVED BY THE CHEMO, THEN NEW SEEDS ARE PLANTED. THEY GROW UP TO BE DEFENDERS, TRANSPORTERS, AND FIX-IT GUYS—JUST LIKE NORMAL!
SOMETIMES, IF THE CHEMO IS NOT ABLE TO KILL ALL THE WEEDS, THE BAD BONE MARROW CAN BE REPLACED BY DOING SOMETHING CALLED A TRANSPLANT.
YOUR BADLY BEHAVING CELLS ARE SWAPPED WITH MAGIC SEEDS FROM SOMEONE ELSE.
THE PROPER MEDICAL TERM IS BONE MARROW TRANSPLANT OR PERIPHERAL STEM CELL TRANSPLANT.
THEN, THE NEW SEEDS GROW INTO NORMAL BABY BLOOD CELLS IN YOUR BONE MARROW GARDEN!
WOW! LOOK AT THEM GROW! THEY ARE SO WELL TRAINED!
AMAZING!
MOST KIDS DON'T NEED TO HAVE RADIATION TREATMENT OR A BONE MARROW TRANSPLANT. IN MOST KIDS, THE CHEMO DOES THE TRICK ALL ON ITS OWN.
DOCTORS ARE NOT SURE WHY LEUKEMIA DEVELOPS IN SOME PEOPLE, BUT YOU'RE NOT IN THIS ALONE! YOUR FAMILY AND THE HOSPITAL STAFF ARE ON YOUR SIDE, AND THEY'RE WORKING HARD TO HELP YOU!

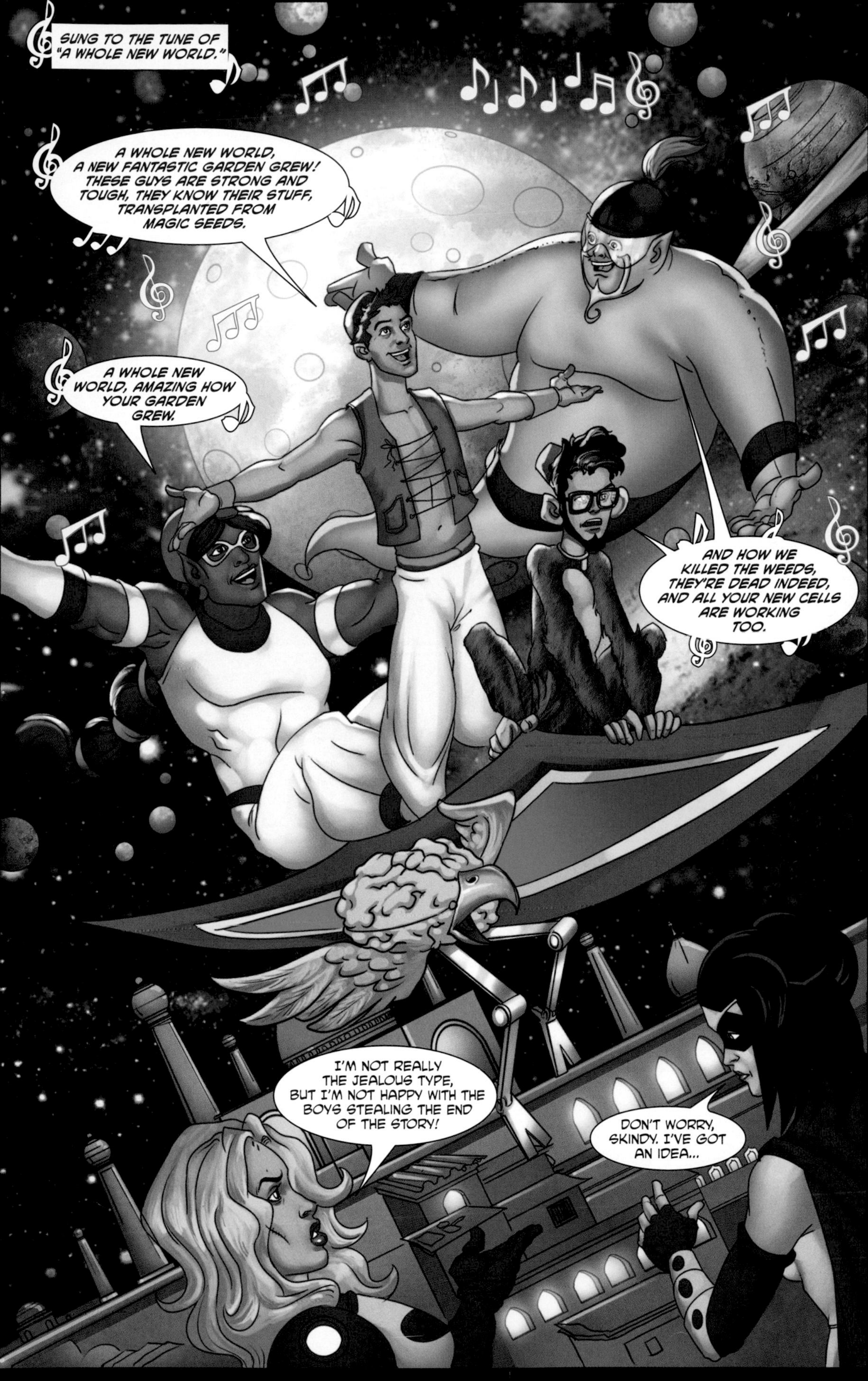
SUNG TO THE TUNE OF "A WHOLE NEW WORLD."
A WHOLE NEW WORLD, A NEW FANTASTIC GARDEN GREW! THESE GUYS ARE STRONG AND TOUGH, THEY KNOW THEIR STUFF, TRANSPLANTED FROM MAGIC SEEDS.
A WHOLE NEW WORLD, AMAZING HOW YOUR GARDEN GREW.
AND HOW WE KILLED THE WEEDS, THEY'RE DEAD INDEED, AND ALL YOUR NEW CELLS ARE WORKING TOO.
I'M NOT REALLY THE JEALOUS TYPE, BUT I'M NOT HAPPY WITH THE BOYS STEALING THE END OF THE STORY!
DON'T WORRY, SKINDY. I'VE GOT AN IDEA...

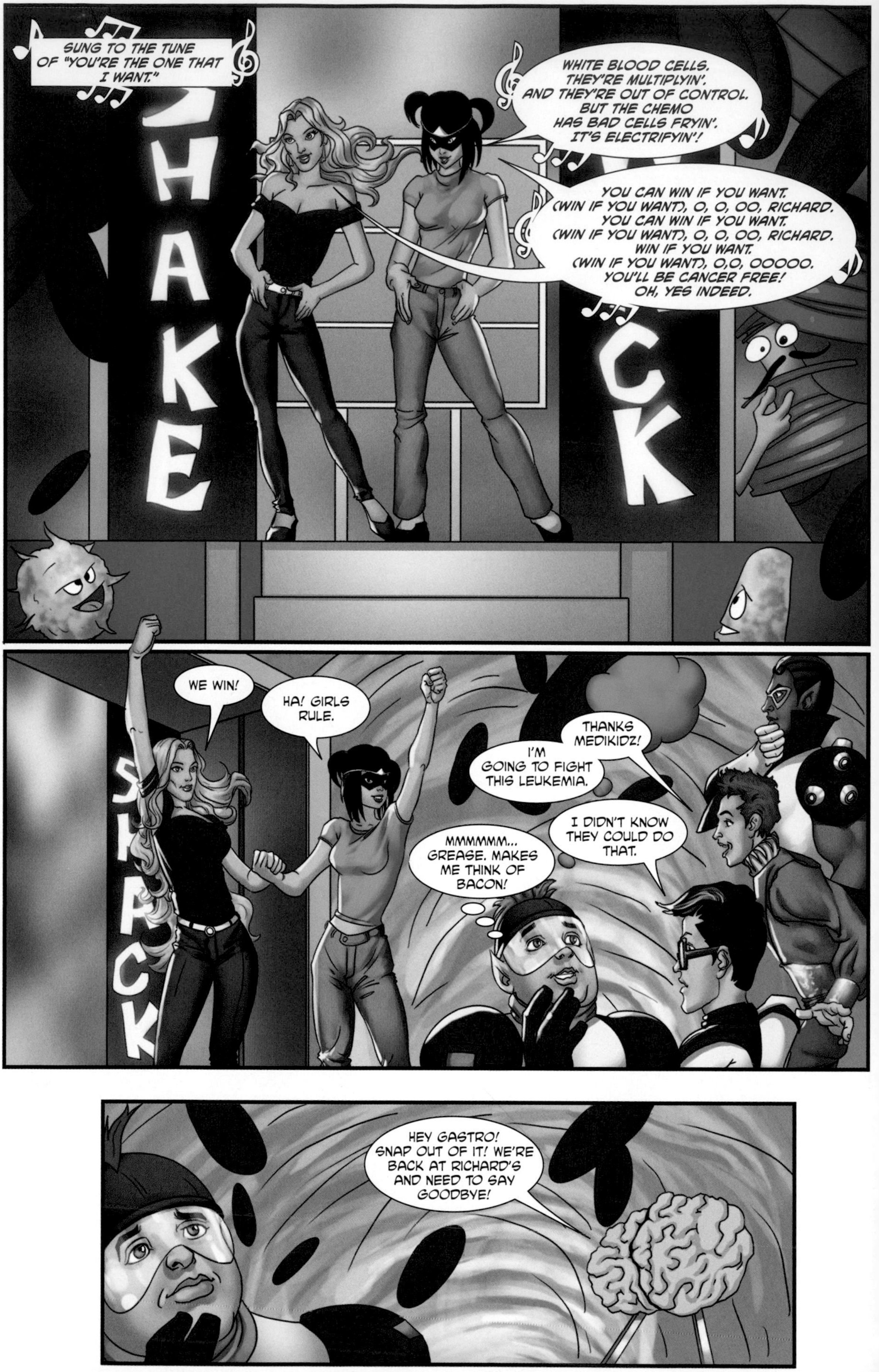
SUNG TO THE TUNE OF "YOU'RE THE ONE THAT I WANT."
WHITE BLOOD CELLS. THEY'RE MULTIPLYIN'. AND THEY'RE OUT OF CONTROL. BUT THE CHEMO HAS BAD CELLS FRYIN'. IT'S ELECTRIFYIN'!
YOU CAN WIN IF YOU WANT. (WIN IF YOU WANT), O, O, OO, RICHARD. YOU CAN WIN IF YOU WANT. (WIN IF YOU WANT), O, O, OO, RICHARD. WIN IF YOU WANT. (WIN IF YOU WANT), O,O, OOOOO. YOU'LL BE CANCER FREE! OH, YES INDEED.
SHAKE
CK
WE WIN!
HA! GIRLS RULE.
THANKS MEDIKIDZ!
I'M GOING TO FIGHT THIS LEUKEMIA.
I DIDN'T KNOW THEY COULD DO THAT.
MMMMMM... GREASE. MAKES ME THINK OF BACON!
HEY GASTRO! SNAP OUT OF IT! WE'RE BACK AT RICHARD'S AND NEED TO SAY GOODBYE!

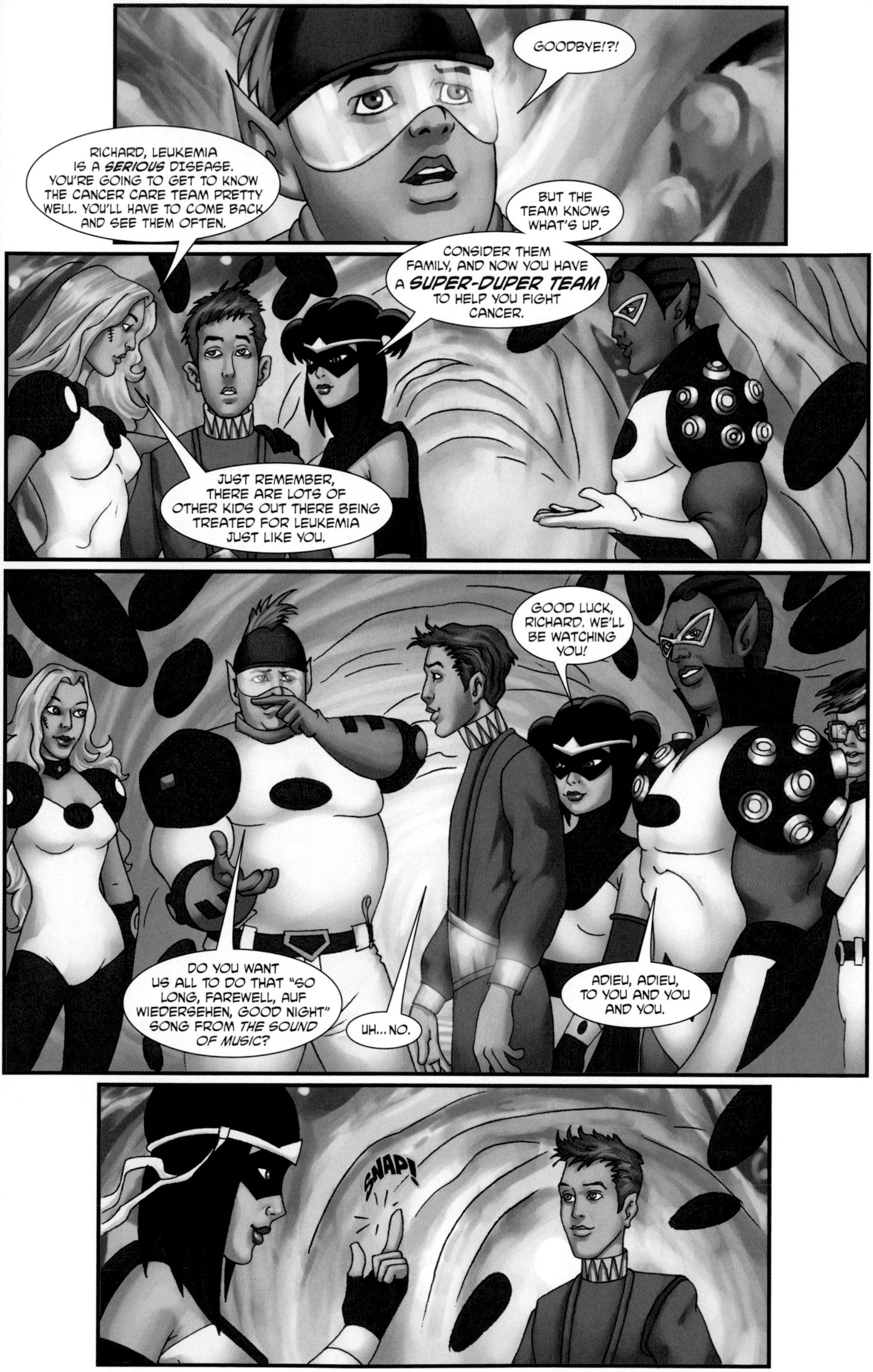
GOODBYE!?!
RICHARD, LEUKEMIA IS A SERIOUS DISEASE. YOU'RE GOING TO GET TO KNOW THE CANCER CARE TEAM PRETTY WELL. YOU'LL HAVE TO COME BACK AND SEE THEM OFTEN.
BUT THE TEAM KNOWS WHAT'S UP.
CONSIDER THEM FAMILY, AND NOW YOU HAVE A SUPER-DUPER TEAM TO HELP YOU FIGHT CANCER.
JUST REMEMBER, THERE ARE LOTS OF OTHER KIDS OUT THERE BEING TREATED FOR LEUKEMIA JUST LIKE YOU.
GOOD LUCK, RICHARD. WE'LL BE WATCHING YOU!
DO YOU WANT US ALL TO DO THAT "SO LONG, FAREWELL, AUF WIEDERSEHEN, GOOD NIGHT" SONG FROM THE SOUND OF MUSIC?
UH... NO.
ADIEU, ADIEU, TO YOU AND YOU AND YOU.
SNAP!

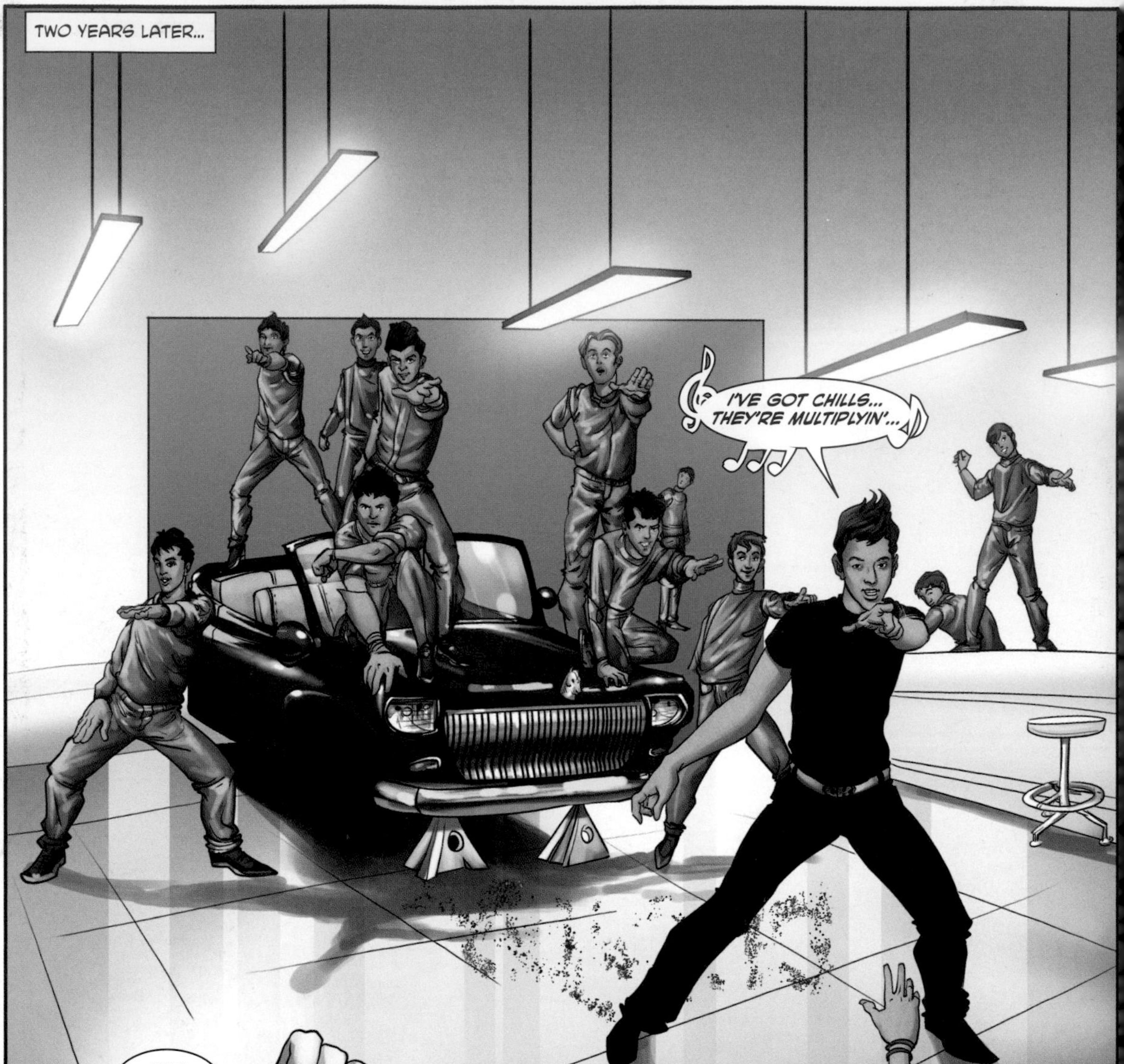
TWO YEARS LATER...
I'VE GOT CHILLS... THEY'RE MULTIPLYIN'...

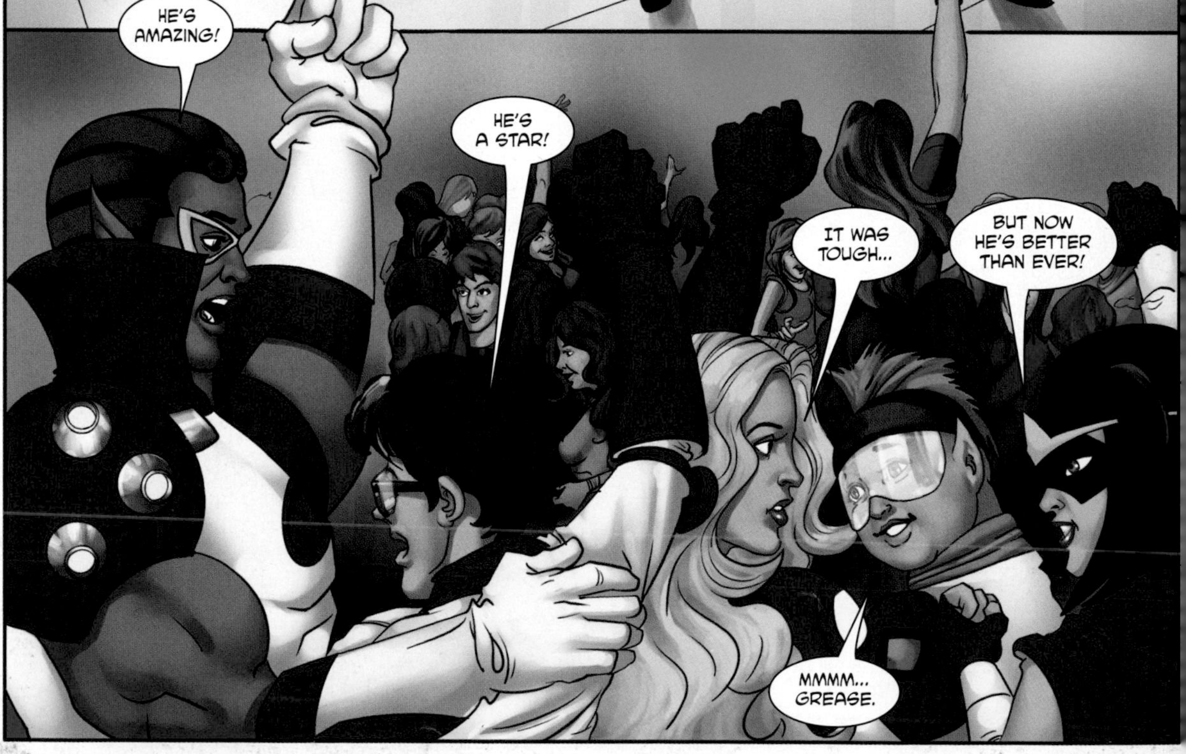
HE'S AMAZING!
HE'S A STAR!
IT WAS TOUGH...
BUT NOW HE'S BETTER THAN EVER!
MMMM... GREASE.